CLARITY

CREATE A HOLISTIC BUSINESS YOU LOVE

CHRISTINE JUDD

CONTENTS

INTRODUCTION

I want to congratulate you for picking up this book. It means you're someone with an amazing gift that the world needs. It also means that you're kinda stuck with getting your gifts out there, finding the people (and trust me they're out there) who need exactly what you have to offer and most importantly make a decent living from it. It's not your fault! Most training programs brush over the business aspects, but hardly any go into detail explaining where to find clients, how to run your books or how to create a website.

It's not their fault either, since they train you in their zone of genius. Most teachers don't hold a business degree, why should they? They are good at what they do.

I do however think training holistic practitioners in business should be much more of a vital part of their training since most of them will end up running their own business. With the internet and social media the world became much smaller, but also much more complex and competitive.

It doesn't matter what modality you've decided on whether that be teaching yoga or Pilates, alternative healing practices such as Reiki, Lomi Lomi massage, acupuncture or anything else. Whether you're just starting your business or have been at it for a while but got stuck and it's not working for you.

This book is a practical guide designed to help YOU get a grasp on how to run your business. I will teach you the do's and don'ts of business, tested tips and tricks so you don't have to experiment and fail (like I did). I want to make it easy for you to live your dream and thrive in your business.

You can use this book any way you want. Start at the beginning, pick the chapters you feel you need right now. There are no rules. You will find my favourite tools that I use to run my business in this book. Yes these will be biased by my own preference, but since I'm kind of a techy nerd, trust me, they're probably the best ones out there. For those who want more options, you will find a more comprehensive list of tools at the end of the book. You will also find exercise prompts in this book that will help you get clarity on various things and will get you thinking about YOUR business. So, get yourself a nice notebook to keep everything in one place.

Before I dive into the book and we start creating your dream life and business, let me back up and tell you a little bit about myself and why I decided to write this book.

Would you believe that if I told you I never wanted to run my own business? It kind of fell into my lap. I studied business, because I didn't know what else to do. It was the path you took, because it's useful and you can do anything you want with it. Or so I was told. I didn't particularly like the course, but finished it anyway. 'Cause that's what you do, isn't it? I ended up getting a job in Marketing for an IT company in Ireland who took a chance with me since I didn't have any work experience. I rather travelled the world in my semester breaks. I learned how to apply what I studied, but I still hated the job, the stress that came with it and thought I generally hated marketing. I should really thank my first boss as he suggested I take up yoga to deal with the stress. That's when my actual journey began. Don't worry, I won't bore you with the details of my self- discovery journey (that's material for another book). Being around so many inspiring and talented people opened up possibilities and showed me that there was another way to live. Far away from the 9- to-5 grind. It was then that a lot of my friends asked me to help them with their websites and marketing. I slowly realised not only that I didn't hate marketing, just the industry I was in, but also that there was a market there that needed my unique talents. Someone who understands both worlds, the business and the holistic, and can bridge the gap between them. That's when my business was born. For years I worked part time on it while still working my day-job, before I took the plunge into full-time Entrepreneurship in 2014. It's been one hell of a journey so far I have to say. Lots of ups and downs, wins and losses, tears of joy and sadness. I'm not going to lie, I've not loved every minute of it, but in the end the good definitely outweighs the bad when it comes to running a business. The freedom of having no one telling you what you should do next, going for a coffee short notice with a friend just because you can and the feeling of unimaginably joy when you earn your first money knowing that it was all you and not just a paycheck, because you showed up.

I've learned a lot along the way, most importantly though that I'm a teacher. I teach myself new things all the time and love seeing the sparkle in people's eyes when they understand a marketing concept, or learn how to use their own website or send out their first newsletter. It's exhilarating. I love interacting with people in my live workshops, but I'm an empath and highly sensitive, so I limit the amount of people in my workshops to a very small number. It gives me the chance to be fully present with the participants and guarantees that they will get attention for their businesses from me.

Unfortunately, it also means I can't reach the amount of people that I know need to learn what I have to teach. That's why I decided to write this book. I sincerely hope you enjoy this book and use it along your own journey as an Entrepreneur sharing your unique gifts with the world.

BONUS TRAINING

This book will provide you will everything you need to know to set up and run your holistic business. I know that sometimes translating the theory into practice can be hard. Especially when it comes to figuring out systems and technology such as email marketing systems.

I believe building your email list is one of THE most important things you can do, which is why I want to give all my readers a special bonus.

I've created an exclusive video course on email marketing just for you. The videos take you step-by-step through everything you need to know, starting with which system to use, how to come up with a freebie to give subscribers in exchange for their email addresses to actually creating that freebie and setting it up in your system. You can claim your bonus from the link below.

http://christinejudd.com/bonus

Make sure to send me links to all your freebies as I always love to see what you create! hello@christinejudd.com

BORING, BUT NECESSARY STUFF

BEFORE WE DIVE in to the nitty-gritty of your business, let's get the boring stuff you need to do out of the way. I will keep this section short and generic. Different countries have different rules. Please make sure to check your countries rules on this. Citizenship information and Tax Office websites usually hold the relevant information.

1. Registering your business name.

Should you decide on using a dedicated business name, rather than your own given name, you will need to register it with the Companies Registration Office.

2. Decide what type of company.

You have several options when setting up your company. Sole Trader/ Sole Proprietor, Partnership or Limited Company. Most Holistic Practitioners start out as Sole Traders or Sole Proprietor which means you're liable to any creditors, but you also get to keep all your income after taxes.

3. Inform your Tax Office.

It is your responsibility to inform the Tax Office that you started trading. As Sole Trader it is also your responsibility to submit and pay your income taxes once a year.

4. Open a dedicated Bank Account.

Once you've got the legalities out of the way and you can open your business bank account. You will need this in order to make it easier to keep your bookkeeping in order.

5. Get insurance.

Whether you are working for yourself or someone else, it is absolutely vital you get Public Liability and Public Indemnity Insurance. I genuinely hope you will never need this, but it is an absolute must.

6.Get started with your bookkeeping.

I know it's my least favorite thing in the world too, but now that you're a business owner, there's no way around it. At the bare minimum, you will need to keep records of your income and expenditures (including invoices & receipts).

2

YOUR VISION

I KNOW this section might come as a surprise to you. What does your vision have to do with running your business you might ask? A lot. Your vision of your life and business is your anchor, the point you can always return to when things get tough. It's your manifesto of why you're doing what you're doing. I also call it your BIG WHY. It will keep you motivated and on track to create a successful business.

Some people come up against a lot of blocks and limiting beliefs when they start this exercise and it can be unbelievably hard to dream up a life you truly want to live. Fear, guilt, shame and self-doubt usually show up big time. We've been raised to believe that our life must look certain ways. Find a job, family and the white picket fence, etc. Only you have the power to break out of the norm and create your dream life. Once you start doing that you will not only face your own fears and doubts but also the disapproval and fears of those around you. That's why having this written down will help you stay on track.

I get dirty looks all the time when people find out I spend at least 4 weeks per year somewhere tropical doing yoga. At first, I've made excuses. Now, I simply smile and say yes, I'm lucky, but I also tell them I have created this life for myself, and so can they. We all have choices. I've made the choice a long time ago that travel is part of my ideal life. Thankfully I have a lot of great people around me who live similar lives and who support me.

I want you to take out a notebook and start dreaming. Because you are dreaming you have all the money, time and experience you need. Anything is possible!

Want to have a 4 hour work day or even week? Done.

Want to work in an amazing, luxurious space? Done.

Want to travel the world while the money is still coming into your bank account? Done.

Want to be a millionaire? Done.

Nothing is too crazy, but I want you to be specific, down to the colour of the picture on the wall. (Mine is a picture of Hawai'i I took last year) Write down how you feel when you're living this life. The following questions will help you get clear on your vision:

- What is it you do?
- Who are you working with or are you working alone?
- Where are you working? What does your work environment look like? Describe the space you are working in in detail e.g. pictures on the wall, colours, accessories
- How many hours are you working every day?
- What is your ideal working day from the time you get up in the morning until you go to bed?
- What does success look like to you? How do you know when you've "made" it?
- How do you feel living your ideal day/life?

- How much do you want to earn? (be realistic on this one as you unfortunately won't make that million Euro the first year)
- Set a time-line for your vision to become reality

Writing down your vision will help you get crystal clear on it, it also creates a pact between yourself and the Universe to manifest this life. That doesn't mean you won't have to take action, but it's a start.

VISION BOARD

What we think, we become. - Buddha

I'm a huge fan of vision boards. I love writing, but I can't deny I'm also a visual and tactile person. If you're like me, you'll love this exercise.

What is a vision board? It's sacred space that displays what you actually want to bring into your life, placing it somewhere you see it often. It's that simple. I have it as my screen-saver on my laptop as I spend a lot of time on it. Every time I open a new application there it is. Essentially, I'm doing small visualizations throughout the day.

According to the popular book The Secret, *"The law of attraction is forming your entire life experience and it is doing that through your thoughts. When you are visualizing, you are emitting a powerful frequency out into the Universe."*

We all know visualizations work. Oprah Winfrey, Will Smith, Jim Carrey all use them. Jim Carrey wrote himself a cheque for $10 million and carried it in his wallet when he was a struggling actor a year before he was hired for his role in Dumb and Dumber. Guess what? He made exactly $10 million from this role. That doesn't mean he sat back and waited for the role to appear out of thin air. He worked at it every single day.

The important thing about creating your vision board is to focus on how you want to feel. Sure, you can add material things to it as well, but I've always found the more I focus on the feeling the better it works. An example from my own vision board is a trip, my trip to Hawai'i I mentioned earlier. I added this trip to my vision board in March 2016. October 2016, I went to Hawai'i for nearly a month.

There are no rules when it comes to creating your vision board. You can add anything you want on it. You can create a big one covering all areas of your life such as relationships, business and finances, home, travel, personal growth (including spirituality, social life, education) and health. Alternatively, you can create one for each section of your life.

The way I like to do it is to have a vision board for long term goals, but then break it down into smaller ones that include immediate, achievable goals that will lead me to the long-term vision. If I only have a long-term board it always feels like having a carrot (or in my case chocolate) hanging in front of you that you can never reach. It gets frustrating and you lose hope that it will ever happen.

HOW DO YOU GO ABOUT CREATING A VISION BOARD?

You can either go old school by getting a big piece of cardboard or cork board, cutting out photos, quotes, sayings, whatever feels right to you from magazines and gluing or pinning them to it.

Or you can use a digital version, like I do. I create all my material in Canva.com. A free online tool that is super easy to use. You can design anything by dragging and dropping images onto your canvas. Canva.com has images available or you can simply use good old reliable Google to find your images.

The most important aspect of your vision board is that it reflects the life you want to create for yourself.

SUCCESS

Let's talk about success for a second. How do you define success? Our society often sees success as having a good job, a house, a car, yadi yada, but is that really true? For some sure, but I think the most important aspect of being successful is being happy. The saying 'Choose a job you love, and you will never have to work a day in your life.' by Confucius comes to mind. For me, this is definitely true. No money in the world can make you happy when you're in a job you hate or feel stuck in your life. I imagine, since you're reading this book, you've already stumbled upon this problem. You know there's more to life than and you're ready to create it. Is there a universal definition of success? I don't think there is. Success takes different shapes and forms for everybody. You just have to figure out what it is to you. Is it working in a field that you love, creating a legacy, raising your children knowing they can achieve anything they want, learning something new every day, knowing your life is filled with abundance, having a big house and a fancy car? Whatever it is, it is YOUR definition. There's no wrong or right in this question.

Sometimes it takes a while to figure this out, and it's also OK to change over time.

3

YOUR BUSINESS IN DETAIL

NOW THAT YOU have a clear vision of how you want your life and business to look like, as well as the legalities of it, it's time to dive in to your business in more detail.

This chapter might feel like we're going on a little self-discovery journey. That's because it all starts with you. Just like you need to be clear on your vision you need to be clear on who you are, what you care about, what values you have and why you're doing what you're doing. I'm talking about the driving force that brought you to where you are today:

Here are some vital questions you need to ask yourself:

- Who are you?
- What are your skills, talents, traits, work experience?
- Ask friends, family, and if you can, customers to tell you what they like about you and what they think you are good at. Don't judge or censor, write down everything they say. What have you overcome yourself?
- What makes you interesting and unique?

- What is your special blend of talents? Why are you doing what you're doing? What are you passionate about?
- What do you care about? What are your values?
- What can people learn from you?
- What do you LOVE to do and would you do it for free?

Why do you need to know this? By now you've probably realised that running a business is not for the faint-hearted. You will need a lot of self-discipline, courage but most importantly passion. There will be times you definitely want to throw in the towel. Believe me, I used to have that thought on a daily basis, but then I remember why I'm doing this. Why I'm so passionate about helping people create their own businesses, why I love teaching yoga and why I've started my Lomi Lomi practice. Without being passionate about what you do, I promise you, you will slowly but surely be eaten up by the pressure of it all. Answering all the above questions will also help you get clear on boundaries (more on that later), the non-negotiables as well as help you get clear on who you want to work with.

I've worked with a lot of Holistic Practitioners and most of them are quite clear on their vision and what they are about. Yet once you bring business into the mix, things can get a bit blurry and messy. They get so bogged down with the reality of running a business that they sometimes lose their passion for their craft. They forget why they started this venture in the first place. Write a manifesto for yourself and keep it in a place you can see it often, so you never lose sight of the big picture. Keep the answers to the above questions in a safe place, you'll need them again at a later stage when you're writing the content of your website. Yes, you'll need one. No, it's not impossible to do.

You might have noticed that I've asked you to answer the question 'What makes you unique?' on your self-discovery journey. The answer to that question will determine the first important marketing concept in your business - your Unique Selling Proposition (USP).

The factor or consideration presented by a seller as the reason that one product or service is different from and better than that of the competition. ∽Entrepreneur.com

Let me translate that into non-marketing speak for you. What makes you different from the person doing the exact same thing as you 200 meters down the road? Why should they choose you over them? What do you have that they don't? You can have two practitioners with identical academic training and practical experience, yet you will choose one person over the other. Why? People connect to people, their energies and experiences. I especially find this to be true when it comes to people's health and well-being. To give you an example. My USP is that I know the industry from both perspectives, the practitioner and the business. I've worked as a yoga teacher for nearly 10 years and have a unique insight into how the industry works, what language people use and how to best reach clients. My USP is determined by a combination of skill sets and experience. Your USP might be subtler than this, it could be the way you teach or help that's different. Think about the benefits your clients get from coming to you, what's the outcome. It could for example be that you provide services in the comfort of their own home and you could say something like 'Complete Relaxation in The Comfort of Your Home'. The fact that they don't have to travel anywhere to get your service can be a USP.

So, if you've struggled to answer the question before, try it again. Think about your experiences, your story and I promise you it, will flow.

4

IDEAL CLIENTS

FINDING out who you want to work with is the most important, yet most difficult thing you'll ever do in your business. It's a concept I introduce to all my students very early on. An ideal client is someone who finds the perfect solution to their problem or needs in exactly what you have to offer. They will be loyal to you, return often and tell all their friends and family about how great you are. Not only that but for you they're super easy to work with and simply light you up.

Often my students only really understand this concept when they've been in business for a while and notice who they don't want to work with. If you've been working with clients already, you'll know what I'm talking about. The ones you dread taking calls from and you rather not make appointments for. Safe to say those will NOT be your ideal clients and you're better off to stay far away from them. Even if that means you're losing out on some income. Trust me, they're not worth your energy and only take up space that's meant to be filled with your ideal clients.

Excluding people is a great starting point. If you already know who you absolutely do not want as your clients. Write it down now. What is it about them that drives you insane? Do they have things in common? Characteristics, gender etc.

There are different approaches to determining your ideal clients. Some use client avatars or personas, outlining the demographics like age, income, duties, hobbies etc. Whereas this can be very useful, in the holistic field I have found a different approach to be more suitable due to the nature of our businesses.

As a Holistic Practitioner, a lot of the times we are trusted with very sensitive physical and emotional problems. Therefore, finding what truly makes our ideal clients tick is vital. We need to know what their biggest challenges are. What keeps them up at night? How would they like to feel? Only then can we start speaking their language and connect with them. One of the biggest mistakes I often see experts (like you) make is not putting themselves into their clients' shoes when they communicate with them. You have to remember that your clients don't understand the medical terms or expert expressions you might be using, they might be in pain and can't even remember the last time they spent a day pain free. Most of the time they don't care about the tools you use to help them. They want to know you understand them, know how they feel right now when they're not well, know what they struggle with. You've gone through a lot of training to get to where you are today and are a few steps ahead of them in your journey. If you're working with people who experience a similar journey to yourself, then try to remember how you felt, what frustrated you, what were you struggling with.

LET ME GIVE YOU AN EXAMPLE OF A NUTRITIONIST.

You could say:

'I work with everyone who wants to be healthier and feel better'.

Not very specific, right? What's their burning desire? Healthier and happier? That can mean a lot of things and is very broad. Who would you market to? The whole world?

If, however you say:

'I work with busy, overwhelmed young moms to create a healthy lifestyle for them and their family'

It's very clear what their struggles & burning desires are.

They struggle with:

- Time management,
- Creating healthy meals for the whole family that don't take up all their time, and
- Knowing what the right kind of nutrition is for themselves and their family.
- Their burning desires are:
- They desperately want to free up time for other things than standing in the kitchen cooking aka save time.
- They want quick & healthy meals that are not complicated to reduce the overwhelm.

Having this clarity on your clients will transform the way you market to people. You know exactly what they're struggling with, what they desperately want in their life. As soon as you know that and communicate it clearly you've won half the battle. We all want to be understood and want help with our struggles. Here are the main questions you want to find the answers to:

- What are their interests and passions?
- What do they struggle with?
- What issues or challenges are they having right now that has them seeking a solution?

- What are their hopes and dreams for themselves and their families?
- What results, or outcomes, do they want?

The good news is you don't have to come up with all of this yourself. The best way to find out what people really struggle with is to ask them. Have conversations with people you think might be your ideal clients. Person to person interviews are a great way to learn what they're struggling with. To get larger amount of data create surveys and send it out to people or post in Facebook groups where you think they will hang out. Typeform.com or Surveymonkey.com are great free tools to create surveys. This type of market research is super important and investing time in doing so will pay out in the long run. Not only do you get a clear trend on what people need, you also get the language they are using which is priceless. We will go through all this in more detail when we look at how to align your vision with reality and conduct some market research.

I know when you're just starting out it can be difficult to get clear on your ideal clients. One thing I have found over the years is that a lot of holistic practitioners end up wanting to help people in similar situations to themselves. For example, for me, I wanted to become a yoga teacher to help other people feel the peace and quiet of the mind that I have experienced. That is one of my main motivations to help people through yoga. For others, it might be that they've struggled with back pain and that's why they want to help people live pain free. Helping people with something you've gone through yourself gives you extra credibility. You're even more relatable and there's an instant trust factor for them, because you KNOW what they're going through first hand. That doesn't mean you you won't trust you if you haven't experienced it, but it does add an extra layer of instant trust.

5

NICHE

CLOSELY LINKED to your ideal clients is your niche. Not everyone will have a niche, but if you can create one for yourself, you will have a much easier time with your marketing.

A niche addresses a group of people with a problem, need or want in common. In a true niche market the issue is not yet or poorly addressed by other companies. Creating a service that serves a niche market means that you're directly speaking to the audience, delivering the exact solution they are looking for.

NICHE = WHO (IDEAL CLIENTS) + WHAT (YOUR SOLUTION)

Let's look at the previous example.

'I work with busy, overwhelmed young moms.' = *IDEAL CLIENT*

Getting healthy can mean a lot of things and isn't very specific or unique. If, however, you add in something more specific that addresses their exact needs you have yourself a niche:

*To provide easy-to-follow nutritional information and quick &
healthy meals for the whole family.' = YOUR SOLUTION*

You can see why this is much easier it and will speak directly to the
hearts and minds of the women in this example. You won't be
wasting any time on scheduling consultations with men or taking
on middle aged women who want to lose weight. Nor will you be
promoting at corporate health fairs. Instead you'll be focusing your
efforts in places they will likely hang out such as Mom and baby
yoga, playtime, Mom clubs etc.

Offering the right solution that you're passionate about is just as
important as finding your ideal clients who are ready for your
solution.

It can feel challenging to narrow down your market and
concentrate on serving this particular population. What if I leave
money on the table? What if I'm alienating other people who I
could also serve?

I can tell you right now, if you've done your research and there are
enough people in the niche for you to serve you will NOT lose out
on income. In fact, you will do the opposite. By specialising in one
area you will be able to establish yourself as an expert, the go-to
person, in this area. Your referrals will skyrocket as people will be
clear on what you do and who you work with. Suddenly you're the
big fish in the small pond, not the small fish in the big pond.

Once you tailor your service to your ideal clients' needs your
marketing will suddenly be laser focused instead of taking the
'throwing everything against the wall and hope something will stick'
approach. Sound familiar? Yeah I know, I've been there myself.

Finding your niche has become a buzz word and can cause a lot of
pressure and frustration for practitioners. Yes, it's great to have a
niche, but sometimes you can't narrow it down to a single problem
or segment of people. And that's OK. If done right, you can serve a

number of niche markets. It will take more time and effort to get known for them and you'll have to be very clear in separating them as not to blur the lines between them. But it can be done.

Niching down just for the sake of it won't work. Unless you're passionate about the solution you're offering, you'll eventually resent just working with one group of people. Don't force it. A niche will present itself.

Deliver YOUR SOLUTION
To the RIGHT PEOPLE
In a UNIQUE WAY.

6

VISION VS. REALITY

DREAMING up your vision is the easy part. Now it's time to see what's already out there and how you differentiate yourself from them. As Holistic Practitioners we don't really like to refer to other people as competitors, but from a business perspective they are. It's important to know who is out there and what they do. Not only will it help you differentiate yourself, but also to learn from them. What do you want to do similar and what do you want to do totally different? I do however, believe that there is space for all of us and different people will resonate with you and not others. There is no reason you can't be friends with other practitioners. There is nothing better than having a community around you of like-minded people who can support you and who you could refer people to who don't fit your ideal client profiles.

Start by looking up Holistic Centre's in your area and who works there in your field. Do they have a website? Then check that out. Or simply google your field and add your city/ area to it. Unfortunately, that won't guarantee that you find them as there are still a lot of practitioners who don't have a website. Shocking I know, but it's a reality. If you're cringing right now, because you don't have one yourself, don't worry I have you covered. Chapter 6 will cover everything you need to know.

Once you've found them, I want you to study them with the following questions in mind:

1. List 5 things you like about them and think they're doing well.
2. List 5 things you don't like and think they are doing badly.
3. What can you learn from them?
4. What services do they offer?
5. How is your product/service going to be different/ better than everything else that is available?

The last question is probably the most important one. Again, sometimes it's just your own life experience that differentiates you from them, but that alone can make a difference for people. Remember, they want to know that you are the right person to help them.

This is not necessarily an exercise you can do once and then forget about it. Aim to look at what other people do maybe once or twice a year, just to be informed. Any more than that and you will fall into the comparison trap. It's not a nice place to be as you'll constantly think, who am I to do this, they are so much better than I, what's the point in even trying. Sound familiar? It is important to know who is out there, but once you know how you differentiate yourself from them, it's important to not dwell on them and get on with things.

Done is better than perfect

We've already touched briefly on getting information on and from your ideal clients. In this chapter I want to dive in a little deeper and help you with exactly what to ask them. You want to find out as much as you can about them and what makes them tick. The more you know, the better you can solve their problems and make sure all your marketing material is directly speaking to them.

You will already have an idea of what you think are their biggest struggles and how they want to feel. Don't be surprised though if they end up telling you something completely different or use completely different language to what you had assumed. Get a big enough sample of people to make sure that it's not just one or two people who are simply looking for something else.

This is the most valuable exercise I have ever done for my own business and that of my clients. Sometimes we knew what they were struggling with but were simply using a completely wrong language and therefore they didn't really know that the service they offered could help them.

There are several categories that you want to learn about.

Demographics

- What is your age?
- What is your Gender?
- What's is your yearly income? (make sure to include the option 'I prefer not to answer')

Challenges and how can you address them

- What's your biggest challenge with regards to __?
- What are your most burning questions about __?
- What are you most struggling with regards to ___?
- How does it feel to be struggling with INSERT THEIR

BIGGEST STRUGGLE? What frustrates you the most about it?

- What have you tried so far to solve INSERT THEIR PROBLEM?
- What do you think you need to really solve INSERT THEIR PROBLEM once and for all?
- If there was a magic fairy who could swoop in and create you the perfect solution, what would it be?
- What do you feel would be possible in your life when you have solved this problem?

Goals

Imagine a life without your biggest struggle. How do you want to feel? What would you do? What would your life look like?

Personality/communication style

- What's your preferred method of learning (reading, listening, watching, practicing, others)
- What blogs or news site do you read?
- What social media platforms do you prefer?
- Tell us a bit about you. What excites you and what makes your blood boil?
- What else would you like us to know?

Objections

What is holding you back from taking the next step to achieve INSERT HOW THEY WANT TO FEEL?

Purchasing Behaviour

Which of the following would influence your decision the most if you were to buy INSERT YOUR SERVICE? Quality, Price, Value, Brand.

People are notoriously short on time. You don't want the survey to take them longer than 15 - 20 minutes. Make sure to cover all the categories and tailor it to your own needs. For more in-depth interviews feel free to use them all and even add your own.

This exercise should only be used for gathering information. Make sure to highlight that you will not be selling them anything. You can add a question in the questionnaire asking them if they wanted to be notified when your service becomes available, but other than that I would be very strict on not trying to sell them something. I would even go as far as entering people into a draw for a little prize as an incentive. Doesn't have to be anything expensive. It could even be a short free consultation or treatment from you.

Industry Research

The last area you need to research is your industry. It is important as it will give you an idea of how big the market is and how many people you can reach with your services. The local statistics office is a good place to start, or if you're in the European Union you can use the Eurostat database which has a lot of useful data from all over Europe. Other sources are government agencies, industry and trade associations, labor unions, media sources, chambers of commerce, and so on. It's usually published in pamphlets, newsletters, trade publications, magazines, and newspapers. Gather whatever information you can find on your industry. You especially want to take a look at the market size, spending behavior etc.

Now that you've dreamt big and have done your market research, you need to do a reality check. It's important to make sure that the industry is big enough and growing? Does it have enough potential clients (and consequently income) available for you to work with? An indication of that is if there are competitors in your area. Yes, competition is actually a good thing. It means there is demand for the service.

Unless you are looking to work in a very specific niche you shouldn't have a problem with your business not being viable.

7

LET'S TALK MONEY

LET'S TALK ABOUT MONEY. I know icky topic for a lot of people. Think of money as an exchange of energy. You are providing a valuable service to people and are receiving energy in form of money in return. I will talk more about this when we get to creating your packages.

But it is important that you have a clear idea of what it will cost you to run your business and it will help you set up your prices at a later stage. If you are living in the EU there are some great financing options for small start-ups.

How much your business will cost to run depends on the type of practice you want to run.

Here are some of your options:

Working from Home

If you have the space to offer your classes or treatments from home is a great option as it will save you costs with regards to space rental, commuting cost etc. Do keep in mind though that you are leaving yourself open to strangers coming in to your home so be careful to set boundaries.

Mobile Practice

Mobile Practices are becoming increasingly popular as people are having busy lives and don't have the time to travel to a space, yet want to still have the benefit of receiving treatments. For you it has the benefit that you can provide individual services without having big overhead costs from room rentals. Downside is that your travel cost will get a lot higher and you will be able to see less clients as you need to factor in travel time.

Hiring a room or space

Hiring a space is a popular option. A lot of people start out renting a room in an established center as it helps with getting yourself out there and piggybacking on existing clients and marketing of the center.

The other option is to fully rent your own space which gives you the chance to run the place exactly how you want it.

Your costs and work load will be the highest if you fully rent your space, but if you have a clear vision of how you want your space to look like, it is the best option.

Working in corporate environment

A lot of corporate companies now are taking up holistic and alternative therapists. It's usually a fairly lucrative place to work as a lot of the time the companies are substituting the treatments for their staff and you can charge good rates. You have a pool of clients directly available to you, but it can take a little time to establish yourself with the employees, especially if you are offering a therapy which they haven't had before.

All of the above options have their pro and cons. It comes down to personal preference.

Your running business costs will depend on which option you choose. I've compiled a list of costs you will need to figure out. Get some different quotes from different providers for insurance, printing etc. It's definitely worth comparing!

Fill them out as best as you can to give you an idea of how much it will cost you to run your business.

Monthly Operating Costs:

Rent _____

Utilities _____

Insurance _____

Internet _____

Phone _____

Transport _____

Heating _____

Bank charges_____

Point of sale charges _____

Advertising _____

Office Supplies _____

Postage & Deliveries _____

Industry Memberships_____

Start up / yearly costs

Office Supplies _____

Equipment _____

Furniture _____

Computer _____

Software   _____

Website   _____

Security Deposit   _____

Marketing   _____

Legal   _____

Accounting   _____

TOTAL :   _____

It's tempting to dive in head first into the adventure, storm in to your boss's office, announce you're quitting and possibly even tell them what you think of them and their job. My advice? Please, don't! Yes, it will temporarily be extremely satisfying. Believe me I wanted to do that a million times over, but hear me out.

My advice to any people starting out as an Entrepreneur and especially Holistic Practitioner is to not quit their day-job just yet. You still need to pay your bills. It will take at least two to three years for your business to be fully up and running and profitable. The pressure is immense to generate that much income when you're starting out. The other reason is that if you've only just finished your training, it will take you some time to find your feet actually doing what you love. If you go full steam ahead you'll be more occupied with running your business than honing your craft. Doing it the slow way, will possibly make you a better practitioner/teacher as you can take your time to overcome these challenges without the pressure of generating a full income.

If you need start-up capital, there are a lot of different funding's and grants available to you. Easiest way to see what's available is to check your local enterprise office. In Ireland and Europe there are a variety of different options available to you. Whether or not you apply for outside financing is a decision you need to make for yourself. Like every loan it has its benefits and drawbacks. It is a good option if you are looking at setting up your own space as you will need a fairly large amount of money to set it up. The other options can be managed without major start-up funding costs as you eliminate some of the costs already.

8

CREATING YOUR PRODUCTS AND SERVICES

NOW THAT YOU have determined what your running expenses are, it's time to look at your own services. What do you offer and what you should charge for them.

For Yoga Teachers and Holistic Practitioners this process is relatively easy, if you are building a traditional business with teaching classes or treating people via various therapies. There are other alternatives like putting together online programs etc. But for now we will be covering the basics.

When you are just starting out it's easy to fall into the trap of giving services away for free, bartering or charging extremely low prices (lower than the standard prices).

I beg you NOT to do that! By doing this you are undervaluing yourself and sending a message to the students/clients that your services are worth less than those who charge. It's about people's perception. People tend to think expensive equals good quality. We all know that's not necessarily true, but wouldn't you rather have people value your services? Of course there are those who are bargain hunters and come when it's free or massively discounted and who will never want to pay full price for a service. Trust me, you don't want those people. You've spent a considerable amount of time training. Nobody would expect to not pay an accountant or doctor. Just keep that in mind.

By setting your prices in the range of market standard, you are sending the message that you are skilled, licensed (where applicable) and most of all professional. You have the skills/training so don't undervalue yourself!

For your convenience, I will split the next section for businesses offering group programs such as yoga teachers and single-client service-based business like massage therapy. So you can skip the section that doesn't apply to you if you like.

Group Programs

You will have (hopefully) thought about this by now already, but let's look at what kind of classes you want to run.

Do you want to run your own classes, offer 4,6 or 8 week courses, private classes or workshops?

Next step is to look at similar structures your competitors run and what they're charging for it. You'll get a feel for what the average is and can go from there.

Classes

Setting class prices slightly depends on how much your costs are for renting the space, transport etc. But generally prices for yoga classes are fairly similar in your city.

You will find it's around the €10-€23/per person mark with a discount if you buy class cards.

Take a look around your city to find out what other teachers/studios are charging and go from there.

Go back to your figures and see how much it will cost you to run a class and this will give you an idea how much you will charge in order to actually make money.

Courses

Running courses generally helps you get bums on seats, get paid in advance and not have to deal with the uncertainty of drop-ins and sitting in front of an empty class room.

Benefits of courses are that you get payment at the beginning of the course.

Usually it's common to set the per hour price a little bit lower than your

drop in rate to give them an incentive to sign up for the full course.

If you're up for it you can allow Drop-ins to the course, but bare in mind that there's the risk of having a complete novice joining in. It's not impossible to do but a bit harder to teach I find.

Class Passes

Offering class passes is a good way of raising your cash flow. Basically you are giving them slight discounts if they buy classes in bulk.

For example:

If your drop in rate is €15 per class. Make it so a 10 class package results in a per class cost less than €15.

A slight note to terms and conditions. Make sure to state them clearly as you don't want someone buying a class pass and trying to redeem it a year later. Give a time frame for how long they are valid for.

Workshops

Workshops are a great way of making a little bit more money per class. It is a lot more work and usually takes time to prepare and are longer.

Pricing on this depends a little bit on your experience, location and length of workshop.

Well-known and long-term teachers are available to charge more. Same as in any other industry.

So for a 2 hour workshop it can range between €20-€60

Again take a look around and compare prices.

Private Lessons

This is a little bit more flexible and you should be earning substantially more than a class rate. It also depends on the economy of the area you work in and your client's budget. Is this a luxury to them that is demanding on their wallet or is the money nothing to them? How qualified are you...beginner or master teacher, somewhere in the middle? Those are determining factors. You can be flexible based on the client's needs, budget, frequency of sessions.

If you want to calculate your hourly rate for a private lesson you will need to calculate the travel time as well.

Create a base rate that you're willing to charge per hour and add your travel time. Here is an example:

=€45(base rate) + calculated travel time (€25/60min=x/40 min of travel time)

=€45 + (€25/60*40=x)

=€45+€17

=€62 for 60 minutes

The base price is just an example and by no means do you have to use it. A good idea is always to offer discounts if they book multiple sessions straight away.

Teaching in Studios

There are 2 different structures yoga studios use

•Fixed rate

Again, to some extend this depends on your experience but standard rates are between €25-€50 per hour

Negotiate with the studio.

Benefit of this model is that if classes are less busy you still get paid the same rate.

Once this changes the studio will make a lot more money on the class, yet you are paid the same.

•Fixed base rate + x€ per student

This is a model that's very popular as you are guaranteed a base rate no matter how many people show up. Usually, the per-head bonus only kicks in after a certain number of students.

For example, you might be paid €20 per class up to ten students, and for every student beyond ten, you get an additional €1-3

It gives you the chance to earn a good per hour rate and an incentive to grow the class.

You can use a similar price structure in Corporates, but I would certainly price your fixed hourly rate higher than in studios.

Single-client service-based business

Your first decision needs to be whether you work for yourself or a spa. There are obvious benefits of having a full-time employment such as stability through secure income, government benefits and no management / marketing responsibility. The trade-off is obviously working for someone else, potentially making less money than you could and not realising your own vision and dream.

Spas

There are 3 different structures spas use.

Fixed salary:

This is like getting any normal job and you get a fixed salary per month. This means you have a steady income but it also limits you with regards to making more money. Salaries vary depending on various factors such as type of spa, your qualifications, experience and location.

Benefit of this model is that if the spa is less busy you still get paid the same rate. Once this changes the spa will make a lot more money on the treatments, yet you are paid the same.

Fixed base rate + x€ per treatment

This is a model that's very popular as you are guaranteed a base rate per hour no matter how many appointments you have. You will then get a commission on each treatment you do. Base rates and commission rates vary but you should at least get minimum wage as your base rate.

Commission

This means that your salary is fully based on commission. This could be anything from 50/50, 60/40 to 70/30 between you and the owner.

Self-employed

As a self-employed Holistic Therapist you have a lot more decisions to make. Starting with what kind of treatments do you offer, how long are your appointments, how much does an appointment cost you, how many hours can you comfortably work without burning yourself out and of course what should you charge for your services?

Pricing your services according to the industry and local standard is important. As I already mentioned you don't want to undervalue your services or yourself. Make sure you are comparing like for like. If a place offers for example a 30-minute Massage and the clients can use their sauna and steam room you can't compare it to a 30-minute Massage you would get at a Holistic Centre without that benefit.

You will need to figure out the minimum cost you need to charge per hour to cover all our expenses. As a sole trader I suggest including your personal bills too to ensure that you've got ALL your bills covered.

How do we go about doing this? Simple, divide all your expenses by the number of scheduled available hours you have per month aka billable hours.

Billable hours are the hours you work in which you are generating income the remaining hours are non- billable hours. For therapists/teachers (and most service providers), this means the hours which you are treating a client.

Non-billable hours include your time spent cleaning up between clients, doing administrative work, and other business tasks no one is paying you for directly.

So, let's say you have an 8 hour work day and calculate 15 mins between treatments that makes for approx. 6 billable hours. 25% of your time will be spent on non-billable hours. If you work 5 days a week that makes 120 hours per month.

This might not actually be a realistic number of hour for you if your work is very physically or mentally draining. You might have to adjust it to what you think/know you can work.

Now take your expenses and divide them by the billable hours you have available in your schedule and you have your minimum price you need to make per hour.

Next step is to calculate the price for your services what % of an hour that service uses.

You now have the minimum price you need to charge to break even. It's time to adjust it to what the standard in the industry is as the minimum price might be considerably lower than that.

The break-even analysis gives you an idea and is a sliding scale depending on how full your schedule is. The less full our schedule is, the more of our income goes towards breaking even. Keep that in mind as especially when you start out you're not likely to have your schedule filled 100%.

It's always good to think about making the experience for your clients special. Adding things like aromatherapy, essential oils or any other extras to your treatment it's perfectly OK to increase your prices slightly.

I know money is a difficult subject especially in this line of business I've started to experiment with what I call the 'What feels right' approach.

Sounds crazy I know, but it makes sure that you are comfortable with the prices and you can raise them over time if they are on the lower spectrum. It takes time to get confidence with regards to pricing.

Now let me warn you this is not based on a scientific rule but more on gut feelings. Here's how you do it!

Set the lowest rate you can possibly imagine working for. (that should be at least the minimum you calculated earlier as otherwise you would lose money!)

Now set a rate that's completely out of your reach. (that should also be relatively in line with the maximum prices in your industry)

Now you have a range to work from so start playing around with numbers in between min/max numbers.

Voila! Not scientific but it has worked for me!

The more your confidence as a practitioner and business owner grows, the more your confidence around money should grow. Remember, money is simply an exchange of energy.

Multi-pack Packages

Getting clients into the door in the first place is probably the hardest part. You will want to make sure they book in with you again. Ideally while they're still with you. Not only does that mean you'll have continuous income you know is coming in, it also means the client will develop a loyalty to you. Let's face it, we're creatures of habit and once we like something we don't want to change. This is your chance to become their practitioner of choice.

Here are some examples of things that work, but be as creative as you want with this.

Buy 5 treatments get one free.

Buy a 10 "pack" of treatments with a $10-$15 discount on each one.

Re-book today and get a discount.

Give "points" for every euro spent redeemable for services, products or discounts.

9

BRANDING

AFTER ALL THE (mostly) boring business stuff we've so far had to deal with it's time for what I think is the best part of creating your business.

A lot of people think your brand is just your logo and colours, but it's so much more than that!

Your brand is the experience you promise to your customers.

- The benefits you commit to delivering. These are things like more time, happiness, relaxation, acceptance, security or pleasure. Does your product or service deliver any of these benefits.
- The promises you make and keep. These include the features your services, and how you deliver them. Do you include extras, or go above and beyond the ordinary? Do you find ways to add value?
- How you follow up after you've delivered. This covers aspects of your business like how you keep in touch, how

> you deal with problems that arise and how you nurture
> your business relationships over time.

It tells them who you are, what you can do for them and how you are different to all the other people out there. Your brand is derived from who you are, who you want to be and who people perceive you to be.

I know creating your brand can feel really daunting. A lot of people in the holistic world are there to serve and help others and creating a brand around that can feel fake or just not right. Especially in today's social media driven world, where we are pressured to present the 'perfect' picture which in reality is just a snapshot of the perfect moments, not the full truth. The real struggle is not about creating your brand, but because you are putting yourself out there, as yourself! You are your brand. In my years of experience, I've found that holistic practitioners or yoga teachers have a strong identity and are in tune with their energy. This is the first step in creating your brand.

That's why staying true to yourself is SO important! People will come to you because of your energy and how you make them feel, not because they really liked the colour of your website or your logo. OK it doesn't hurt to have something visually appealing but it's the whole package that needs to fit.

Looks will draw them in, but what will truly capture them is YOU and your personality.

There are different aspects that define a brand such as brand personality, brand voice and brand identity. All of these make up your brand.

Brand Personality

Your brand personality gives your clients something they can relate to. It's assigning human traits and qualities to your brand. Think back, what's your driving force behind what you do? How do you describe your business to other people? What adjectives do you use to describe your business? What qualities do you want your ideal clients to associate with your business? All these questions will help you derive your brand personality. As you develop, so does your brand. Since what we do is closely linked to personal and spiritual development your brand will most likely develop over time and you will add or take away traits that no longer serve you. We're multi-faceted beings and so is your brand. We have both light and shadow, yin and yang, positive and negative in us. Whereas yes, we want to highlight the positive aspects, but don't forget to look at the negative too.

It can be challenging to come up with positive adjectives. Often in my workshops I get my students to start with what they absolutely do not want to be associated with them and their business. From there you can flip it around and create the positive.

If you're absolutely struggling coming up with adjectives here are some examples:

Positive adjectives

adaptable, adorable, agreeable, amusing, boundless, brave, bright, calm, capable, charming, cheerful, confident, courageous, credible, dazzling, decisive, delightful, determined, dynamic, eager, efficient, encouraging, enduring, energetic, enthusiastic, excitable, fabulous, fair, faithful, fantastic, fearless, friendly, funny, generous, gentle, good, happy, harmonious, helpful, hilarious, honorable, impartial, industrious, instinctive, jolly, joyous, kind, kind-hearted, knowledgeable, likable, lively, lovely, loving, lucky, mature, modern, nice, obedient, painstaking, peaceful, perfect, placid, plausible, pleasant, plucky, productive, protective, proud, punctual, quiet, receptive, reflective, relieved, resolute, responsible, righteous, romantic, sedate, selective, self-assured, sensitive, shrewd, silly, sincere, skillful, splendid, steadfast, stimulating, talented, thoughtful, thrifty, tough, trustworthy, unbiased, unusual, upbeat, vigorous, vivacious, warm, willing, wise, witty, wonderful, zany, zealous.

Negative Adjectives

abrasive, abrupt, abusive, aloof, ambiguous, angry, annoyed, anxious, arrogant, awful, bad, belligerent, boorish, boring, callous, careless, clumsy, combative, confused, cowardly, crazy, creepy, cruel, cynical, dangerous, deceitful, defective, defiant, depressed, deranged, disagreeable, disillusioned, disturbed, domineering, draconian, embarrassing, envious, erratic, evasive, evil, fanatical, fierce, finicky, flashy, flippant, foolish, forgetful, frantic, fretful, frightened, furtive, greedy, grieving, grouchy, gruesome, grumpy, guarded, gullible, helpless, hesitant, horrible, hurtful, ignorant, irresolute, jealous, jittery, lacking, lazy, lonely, malicious, materialistic, mean, mysterious, naive, nasty, naughty, nervous, noisy, obnoxious, outrageous, over, zealous, panicky, pathetic, possessive, quarrelsome, repulsive, ruthless, sad, scary, secretive, selfish, silly, slow, sneaky, snobbish, spendthrift, squeamish, stingy, strange, sulky, tacky, tense, terrible, testy, thick-skinned, thoughtless, threatening, tight, timid, tired, tiresome, troubled, truculent, typical, uptight, vague, vengeful, venomous, volatile, voracious, vulgar, wary, wasteful, weak, wicked, worthless, wretched.

Have you got your list ready? Good, keep it somewhere safe. We'll need it again later.

Brand Voice

From your brand personality derives your unique brand voice. You are unique! No one else is like you! So, your voice will be unique too. Brand voice looks at the tone of your communications and style of writing. Every email, blog post, Facebook post needs to reflect your own brand voice. However, like anything in your business, it's not really about you. It's about your clients. They are as unique as you in terms of experiences, belief systems and personality. You have to find a middle ground between how your audience is speaking and staying true to yourself.

By now you should have done some market research and hopefully gotten some good information on your clients. How do they talk? Are they formal and precise? Or casual and conversational? What's their attitude? You want to appeal to them, so using formal and stiff language and sentence structure will not work if you're trying to appeal to a young, cool and informal speaking audience.

Let me give you an example of my out of office reply that I have always on to manage people's expectations. Yes, even there your brand needs to be portrait.

Hey,

thanks so much for your email. It has arrived safely in my inbox.

Due to the nature of my business, I'm not always at my desk, but I will respond to your email as soon as I can.

If you want to learn more about my services, feel free to check out my website christinejudd.com

It's informal but not disrespectful, personal, casual and uses simple language.

Compare this to a Formal, authoritative and serious approach usually used in corporate settings:

Greetings,

Thank you for your inquiry. A member of our team will respond to you within 2-3 business days.

Can you see the difference?

Check back in with your competitors. Take a look at them and analyse their voice. Then figure out what you like and might adopt and what not.

You have looked at your customers and ideal clients. It's time to look at YOUR own voice. You've looked at phrases earlier, dig them out and start defining your own voice. Don't worry if you don't nail it straight away. You can always go back and tweak it.

I've compiled some examples of opposite brand voices for you to get started.

Fun _____ Serious

Casual _____ Formal

Relaxed _____ Professional

Modern _____ Traditional

Youthful _____ Mature

Unique _____ Familiar

Formal _____ Conversational

Humble _____ Bold

Complex _____ Simple

Educate _____ Entertain

Inform _____ Sell

Warm _____ Authoritative

Now that you have some idea I want you to narrow it down to **three words** that capture the personality of the voice you want for your brand. Then limit those words with three more words. Something like:

Bold, but not arrogant.

Irreverent, but not offensive.

Loud, but not obnoxious.

Brand Identity

We're finally getting to the part that most people associate with branding. The visible elements of a brand. The look and feel of things. I love this part of the business creation. You can finally get visual and let your creativity run wild!

A Brand identity consists of several unique identifiers:

Colour – Warm colours are happy and stimulating; cool colours are more relaxed and calm

Typography – Serif typefaces are formal and mature; sans serifs (which are used on most websites) are more agreeable and modern

Images – People connect strongly with photos that include faces; landscapes leave more room for user interpretation

Shape – Hard edges are more formal; round elements are casual

Logo - A logo is a recognisable and distinctive design. It can include a symbol or a stylised name. If you can relate your symbol to your area of expertise it will make it easier for people to know what you to. If you are an acupuncturist you could consider using symbols that reflect your field such as the needle or the outlines of a body. A Herbalist could use flowers and medicine bottles. You get the idea.

You can find inspiration anywhere in Magazines, websites you like, nature etc. Personally, Pinterest is my first resource for anything brand related. Creating a 'brand' board (like a vision board) with everything that resonates with your brand personality and voice is the first step. Images, fonts you like, textures anything you can think of. It will help your designer immensely in creating your logo and your mood board, which basically is your brand identity at a glance. Including logo, typography, colours, textures and feature images.

A word of warning before you dive into it though. Hiring a designer to do your brand identity can cost anything between €50 and €5000. There's definitely something to be said about spending money on your branding, however if you're just starting out I would not go full out and spend a fortune on branding. Of course, it's up to you, but I have seen a lot of people starting out spend money on branding only to realise a short while later that it's not who they are or want to be in their business. To start out with sites like fiverr.com or 99designs.com have amazing designers who can deliver logos and basic brand identities. As I said earlier your business and brand develops over time. Every business goes through an evolution. Just google some brands and see how their brand identity has changed overtime.

Working with a designer is a process and an experience in itself. You're expecting someone to translate what's visually in your head. They're not mind readers. The more precise your brief to them is the better. Once you've decided on a designer, make sure you know exactly what you're getting. How many revisions of your logo will he/she do? Does the package include a social media package? Will you get the design files?

You'll want to make sure to get the design file or vector file of your logo. This will ensure that if you create big designs like banners or window stickers your logo will appear sharp and not blurry.

Branding is about consistency across anything you do, not only visually. Ideally you want to print out your brand personality, brand voice and brand identity and stick it somewhere you will see it whenever you work on your business. Before you do or post anything. Check back in. Does it fit in with your brand or not?

10

WHAT MAKES A GOOD WEBSITE

PROBABLY ONE OF the questions I get asked the most by people is: Do I need a website? In my opinion, absolutely. Think about it. What's the first thing you do when you hear a recommendation for something? I don't know about you, but I check out their website. Not having a website, to me, says unprofessional. I get that it's overwhelming. The cost, the tech, the fear of being visible, the panic about what to actually put on it. I find that especially for yoga teachers and holistic practitioners the tech side of business can be particular scary.

A one-page website can be enough as long as you capture their attention and tell them what they need to know. Did you know that you only have approximately 7 seconds or less to convince them that you and your offers are the answers to their prayers? Make it count!

The number one tip I can give you is to design your website with your ideal client in mind. You could have the best content for them but if it's buried in a badly designed website that's hard to navigate and they can't find anything they are going to move on.

To create a great website, you need to put yourself in the shoes of a first time visitor and most importantly your ideal clients. What are they looking for?

They want to know WHO you are and WHAT do you do and HOW you can help them solve their problem. You know who your ideal clients are, know their problems, what are they thinking, how are they communicating, etc. It's time to put everything we already talked about so far into action.

It's your chance to build an emotional connection with them, bring your personally in and let them know that you understand what they're struggling with/going through. You KNOW what they need and you need to convince them that YOU are the right person to help them with their problems.

People are drawn to energies and personalities more than they are to a particular product. So, let your personality shine through in your website and let them see who you are.

Guide your visitors through your site. In other words, tell them what they want to know. Who you are and most importantly how working with you will solve their problems. After that tell them what to do next.

Remember, you're here to answer the prayers of your clients. You are setting the tone of your brand and a lot of the times it's the first time they encounter you. They've been searching for someone to help them fix whatever their biggest problem is for such a long time. Don't make them search around for it. Make it easy and clear for them to find what they're looking for and take action to work with you.

There was a time when it was enough to create a static website and add a form 'Sign up to our Newsletter'. More bad news...it no longer is. Your website is a one-stop-shop for people to get to know you, learn about your services but also an opportunity to grow your email list and sell something 24/7. The dream of money coming in while you're sleeping or sipping cocktails at the pool has become extremely popular. Creating alternative incomes streams away from classes and treatments is a topic that deserves its own chapter so we'll be covering this a little later.

MOST IMPORTANT PAGES OF YOUR WEBSITE

Let's look at the most important pages individually and how I go about creating a website.

It might be counter intuitive, but DON'T start with your homepage. Your homepage is like the topping on your ice-cream. Do you eat the rest of the ice-cream if the topping is not to your liking? Of course not! The topping is what you see and eat first and if you don't like it you won't eat the rest, no matter how good it is. The same is true for your homepage. So, leave that for last.

Start with the easiest of them all your:

CONTACT PAGE

The minimum information you should have on here would be your contact details such as phone number, email address, address if you have one for your business maybe in form of a map and a contact form.

You might think you can't add any personality to your contact page, but this is where you can really stand out from the crowd.

No one wants to read the usual. 'Contact me to find out more about my services. Everyone does that.' Stand out and remind them of your personality.

Why not try something like this 'Want to work with me? AWESOME I can't wait!

All you need to do is drop me a line and tell me about how amazing you are and what's bugging you and we will get right on it to fix that.'

That's obviously a informal language but you get what I mean. Use the work you've done on your brand voice and really let it shine.

Your contact page is also the place to remind them of all the other ways they can connect with you such as social media channels.

Maybe something like:

Wanna hang out with me some more? Jump over Instagram, Facebook etc and to see what I'm up to.

ABOUT PAGE

Apart from the Homepage this is the most visited page on a website. People want to get to know you. They want to get a feel of who you are and if you could be the one to help them.

The one thing that is absolutely necessary for this page is a professional picture of yourself. A selfie taken with your phone won't cut it. It simply doesn't look professional. Believe me I know how scary it is to put yourself out there and add your face on the internet. You can read people and their energies from a picture. People will trust you quicker so it's definitely worth investing in a professional photo session. I know I struggled with it, but I can honestly say that it is the change I made to my website that made the biggest impact. Photographers know how to make you look good, so even if you feel like you're not photogenic at all, I promise you the pictures will look great!

You might think that the about you page is all about you, what trainings you've done etc. It is and it isn't. It's about telling your story of how you got to where you are today, but more in terms of why you do what you do. Most people don't really care about lists of certificates you've accumulated. They care about your story and whether or not they connect with it and you.

What have you overcome yourself? What makes you interesting and unique? What is your special blend of talents?

Most importantly though do you understand them and their struggles?

You want to tell them why exactly YOU are the right person they should trust with their biggest problem. It's again more about them than you. You're trying to build trust and make them feel understood by you and realise that you and no-one else is the person for the job.

Tell your story, be yourself and connect with them, but don't forget to tell them what to do next. You've gotten their trust now and they want to work with you. Make it easy for them and tell them how they can do it right on this page. Add a call to action to the page. Book an appointment, consultation or class with you. Whatever it is you want them to do next.

WORK WITH ME / SERVICES PAGE

People will most likely get there, because they've liked what you've written so far.

The battle is half won!

Now remember you are the expert in your field, but your ideal clients are not, so don't us any jargon that they don't understand.

Keep it simple and write as if you're explaining it to someone completely new. If you have done the survey look at the language your clients used and incorporate it. Keep it short and sweet as people have short attention spans.

There are different ways to structure this page depending on whether you offer just one service or multiple different modalities.

ONE SERVICE

Start with:

I DO THIS: explain in simple language what you do. Keep it short & to the point

SO THAT: tell them why the services you provide benefit them

BECAUSE : why you care / what's your drive

The next section will look at who this is for and who it is not. Be clear on this as it will avoid non-ideal clients getting in touch with you and wasting your time! You could start with 'This is for you, if...' or ' If you are struggling with...'

Now put these blurbs together and you have your what, who, how, why.

Now tell them to book in with you.

Break your page up with (high quality) images and paragraphs, it will help the reader to easily understand your page.

MULTIPLE SERVICES

A lot of holistic practitioners will have multiple services they offer for example Massage, Reiki & Reflexology. In that case I would add a box for each therapy an image and an explanation that covers the benefits and features of this modality.

If your modality is not very well known or complicated and needs explanation it's worth considering creating an extra page for it and follow the single service structure from above. People might not be familiar with it and you want to make things easy and clear for them. You can still add it to the overview page and use 'Learn more' as a call to action for it.

Your Work with me page is a good place to add in some testimonials. Written are good but video are golden. What's a better way to tell people how great you are than coming directly from your clients? Testimonials give you credibility and re- assure your future clients you are who you say you are.

Once the know how they can work with you, you have built credibility now it's time to give them one (and only one!) thing to do.

Think words like

SIGN UP / SCHEDULE / MAKE A RESERVATION

PRICING

Let's talk pricing. Should you put your prices on your website? There are different views on it, but my personal opinion is a definite yes. Be transparent about your prices. There is no reason to hide your prices. People's perception if you hide your prices will be that you're too expensive and they can't afford you anyway. Your ideal clients will have no problem paying the price you charge. The ones who won't are not likely clients you want anyway.

While we're on the topic of money, make it easy for people to pay you. Even if you are running a holistic practice where you actually see people (rather than offering online services) consider offering online payments. Tools like PayPal or Stripe make it very easy for people to pay you securely online. Cashless payments are becoming more and more common and the way the world is going we might have a cashless society in a few years. Yes, there's a cost involved in taking payments, but you can expense it. It means clients have ease of mind and don't have to worry about bringing cash to the session, but it also means that in case they cancel, you won't be out of pocket.

FAQ / TERMS OF CONDITIONS PAGE

People always have questions, even if you have answered them on your website in different areas. To avoid having all those flooding in by email consider creating a page.

This is an excellent place to tackle all those questions people might have on how you work and you can refer people to it to. Here are some examples:

How long are your sessions? Are they suitable for me?

Do I need to bring anything? What's the cancellation policy? Will I get a refund?

Stating these things clearly on your website will avoid any problems when it comes to payments. You're clearly stating what your policies are and can refer people to it.

HOMEPAGE

It's the most important page you will create apart from your about page. The easiest way to explain how to structure a homepage is by using the simple, yet powerful marketing concept called AIDA.

AIDA stands for Attention, Interest, Desire and Action. Grab their ATTENTION:

The easiest way to do this is by using imagery and a strong headline that addresses their problems and summarizes what it is they'll be getting on the page. If you're the face of to include an image of yourself as people will get to know and connect with you already.

Spike their INTEREST:

You've got the attention, now it is time to ensure it is interesting for them to stick around. People are strange creatures...they don't want to be presented with the end result but usually identify better with their problems.

Present them with their problems...Asking questions or statements they can identify with is always a good thing. Here are some examples of my own site

You are brilliant in what you're doing and have great visions but are struggling to bring them to life?

You are overwhelmed by all the hats you have to wear as an entrepreneur?

You want to be empowered to all things social media related (even if eventually you choose not to!)?

You pull out your hair and throw a tantrum whenever you have to think about websites or any other tech systems?

FUEL THEIR DESIRE

Now that they identified themselves it's time to show them how you can solve their problems. It's all about making them see how your products/services will solve EXACTLY those problems you've identified....not only that though, but also why YOU are the best person for the job...So here are the questions you need to answer for that section:

How exactly are you going to help them solve their problems? Who are you what makes you unique? AKA what's your unique selling point?

This section is also about building trust with your audience...so slipping in some testimonials or publications you've been featured in and a picture of yourself will help build trust!

HOLD THEIR HAND TO TAKE ACTION

A lot people stop there and lose out on potential business. Adding a 'Call to Action' to every page is your change to guide your potential customers to where you want them to go and what you want them to do next. You really need to hold their hand and tell them what to do.

Do you want them to book in for a discovery call, book in to one of your classes or check out your services in more detail or download your free resource you created that helps them solve their biggest issue? Don't over-complicate, make it prominent and easy to understand.

Think phrases like

- Download my free eBook now
- Sign up to a free trial
- Schedule an appointment

You will have noticed that most pages will have a call to action. Think about it, what if they don't land on your homepage but on a blog post you've written? You don't want to lose them, right? You want them to check out your services, or download a guide you created for the topic they just read about. In other words, you want them to fall in love with you and everything you have to offer.

BLOGGING

Let's talk about your blog for a minute. You might not want to hear this, but you will need to continue to continuously create content.

Unfortunately, the times when it was enough to just have a website that tells people who you are and what you do are over. If you want to stand out and establish yourself as an expert you need to share the knowledge. Not only that, Google rewards you for adding new content to your website, but giving you higher ranking which means you'll be further up on the search results. They no longer put a lot of emphasis on keywords.

Your blog, or call it content if you don't like the word, will give people the chance to get to know you on a continuous basis. You can create loyal followers by giving them useful information all the time. You can also use it as a reference to refer people to. As yoga teacher for example one of the question that comes up all the time is: 'Do I have to be flexible?' Answer their question, but how good would it be if you had a resource such as a blog post you can refer them to and say to them 'I've actually written about this in more detail, here's the link feel free to check it out.' I'll talk you through how to create content in the next chapter.

11

DESIGN TIPS

THE DESIGN of your website is a personal preference, but there are some things you should consider. From a design point of view here are some pointers of what makes a powerful website:

COHERENT DESIGN CHOICES.

Pre-formatting in templates has a reason! Make sure that ALL your pages should look like they belong together. Make sure your fonts, font sizing, fonts, and colours are all consistent. Go back to your branding guide and use that to make sure you stay consistent!

DON'T HIDE KEY INFORMATION.

On every page in your website, key information, aka what they really want to know, should be "above the fold," meaning that the user shouldn't have to scroll around the page to find them.

EASY TO USE NAVIGATION.

There are a handful of different navigational structures and menu types in website design. Don't try to be unique by re-inventing the wheel. Stick to them otherwise you will just confuse people as they have to think about how to use your website and chances are you have already lost them and it distracts from your message.

UNCONVENTIONAL VS CONVENTIONAL

Avoid unconventional colours.

Lots of people want to think "outside the box" when it comes to website design, but you have to be careful when it comes to colour choices.

There's only a slight difference between something that makes your pages "pop" and colouring that's distracting and irritating to visitors.

HIGH QUALITY GRAPHICS

Please use high quality graphics. It is SO important. Think about it. What are you attracted by? Most likely nice imagery and not some blurry images or dare I say clipart.

Good websites for high quality images are Unsplash.com, pixabay.com, freeimages.com, all- free-download.com, fotalia.com, www.istockphoto.com, www.shutterstock.com. The first three are free.

READABLE FONTS

Fonts are also a big part of the picture. Make sure to use easy to read fonts. Keep that in mind when working with your designer on branding. Any good ones will know this anyway!

Swirly fonts are not your friend! Make the font big enough for people to read. Make sure to use fonts that are displayed correctly by all web browsers and mobile devices.

MOBILE COMPATIBILITY

More than half of all web users access the Internet through tablets and smart phones. If your webpages don't display properly for them, then you can't be surprised when you aren't getting the kinds of results you planned for. Also, Google now penalizes you for not having a mobile responsive website by shoving you down to the end of the search results.

CONTENT FORMATTING

Think about how you like to read text. Would you prefer one big bulk of text or rather have it split up in logic paragraphs? Start using more formatting, subheadings, cut paragraphs & use bullets/numbers and highlight important words/phrases. People who scan your website will see and recognise these words.

- Contrast. Make sure that your copy is darker than the background or other way around. Important parts such as buttons or call to actions should stand out.
- Line-height. Set line-height from 1.5 to 1.75 to ensure that lines have enough space to breathe and are perceived as a clean layout.
- Hierarchy. Visual hierarchy is a concept of drawing emphasis on certain elements and establishing a structure with more important elements over others.

Systemize your copy, most of the people now scan online so make it easier for them by using noticeable headlines, sub- headlines, bullet points.

12

CREATING CONTENT TO ATTRACT YOUR IDEAL CLIENTS

THE BAD NEWS is you'll need to create content. The good news is it doesn't mean you have to write the content. To some writing comes more naturally than to others. Thankfully you have other options such as audio or video. Audios and podcasts are a great way to learn things on the go, while walking, doing housework, during the commute. Videos are great for showing people how to do things, hold interviews or show behind the scene footage. You can easily get your audio or video file transcribed using websites like fiverr.com or rev.com

For me, writing is a lot easier than getting in front of the camera. The way marketing is going through, video will become more and more necessary and we all will have to get over our fear of video. Social media platforms like Facebook make it very easy to use video with their Facebook Live feature. It not only depends on your preference of how to create content but also on how your clients want to consume content. Some businesses offer all three variations to their clients to make it easy for everyone to consume content and learn best.

You don't need professional equipment to start out with. Your smartphone or pc will work perfectly. The only equipment I recommend getting is a tripod and a microphone and if you want the audio quality to be outstanding.

Creating content brings up a lot of fears for people. I can already hear the self-doubt and uncertainty arise in you right now. Who am I to write about this topic? I have no idea what to write about! Everything has already been written about! I have no time to create content. I get it. It's not easy and I've certainly been there myself. But one thing that always brings me back down to earth is the fact that I know more about things I do than my clients or students. You only have to be one step ahead of them to help them with something. Don't forget, you've been through hours and hours of training to become a professional in your field so I guarantee you, you are qualified to talk about your field of study. After reading this chapter you will also no longer have the excuse to not know what to write about.

Before we dive in to create your content calendar, let's briefly look at how often you should blog. There is no definite answer to that question, but quality is definitely better than quantity. If you create one highly valuable post a month and re-use and re-distribute the content widely that can be enough. Others find they can produce content every other week or even weekly. The key is consistency.

In fact, I can fill a content calendar for year in less than an hour! Don't believe me? Try this exercise using mind maps.

I tend to go old school on my mind maps and use pen and colourful paper. You can also use things like mindmeister.com or mindmup.com. Either will work fine.

Step 1: Come up with different categories you want to write about.

Let's take my business as an example. My categories are:

- Yoga
- Holistic Marketing / Tech Bites
- Hawaiian Culture & Healing
- Running a biz
- If you run a yoga business it could be:
- Yoga Postures
- Yoga Philosophy
- Breathwork or Pranayama
- Yoga Lifestyle

I usually have 4 categories as it fits nicely with 4 weeks in a month and you'll end up with one blog post per week when you rotate the categories.

Add those categories each in a circle on your piece of paper or the online version.

Step 2: Brainstorm things you want to write about within that topic.

The wonders of the internet provide you with plenty of inspiration for this.

Sites like http://answerthepublic.com or Google Trends are a tremendous help in coming up with a lot of different ideas people are actually searching for. If you want to come up with topics yourself without the help of the world wide web consider these prompts to come up with ideas. Let's use the yoga example again but you can replace YOGA with your category or topic.

YOGA + LIFE: Yoga changed my life forever for the better.

YOGA + KIDS: What my kids have taught me about `yoga.

YOGA + CAREER: The full story of my career in `yoga.

YOGA + MONEY: How much money does `yoga make?

YOGA + FRIENDS: My friends didn't understand `yoga at first, but then I told them this...

YOGA + LOVE: How `yoga affected my love life.

YOGA + TUTORIAL: How to `yoga like a Rockstar.

YOGA + EMOTIONAL SIDE: When I started `yoga I was scared to death...

YOGA + TECHNICAL SKILL: Here's how Photoshop can improve your `yoga performance.

YOGA + FEARS: For a full month I would wake up every night having nightmares about `yoga.

YOGA + TOOLS/HACKS: 12 years of `yoga experience and here's the top 3 things I've learned.

When it comes to blog titles there are some useful formulas that always good responses. Here are some examples.

1. Number + Adjective + Noun + Keyword + Promise

5 simple tips to us create a daily yoga practice in less than a month.

2. How to + Action + Keyword + Promise

How to create a daily yoga practice in a month.

3. Definition + Guide to + Action + Keyword + Promise

The complete guide to creating a powerful daily yoga practice in less than a month.

4. Negative Word + Action + Keyword

Stop worrying about your belly jiggle and start practicing yoga using these 5 tips.

5. How to ____.

6. How to ____ in X Steps.

7. X Simple Secrets You Didn't Know About ____.

8. X Lies You've Been Told About ____.

9. X Myths About ____ You Probably Still Believe.

10. The One Thing You've Been Missing to ____.

11. Why We Love ____ (and You Should Too!)

12. The Beginner's Guide to ____.

13. Top 5 tips to ___.

14. How to ___ right away.

You get the idea. It's easier than you think.

Step 3: Create a calendar

This step is the easiest. All you have to do is put everything together in a calendar or a spreadsheet. Add the category, title, publish date, call to action used in as the basics.

I mentioned that consistency is the key to being successful not only with blogging but with marketing in general. A great way to stay consistent is to batch your content. Rather than having the pressure of having to create content every week, dedicate half a day or a day on creating your content for the month and schedule them to be published on the same day every week throughout the month. Rather than creating a new different looking feature graphic for each blog post create a template in Canva.com where you just had to change the title. It will make your blog overview page look consistent and people will start to recognize your brand. I know whenever I do it, it keeps me on track.

We'll cover how you can use all this content you create as part of your marketing strategy in the next chapter.

13

SUSTAINABLE BUSINESS STRATEGY

YOU'VE GOT YOUR VISION, ideal clients, brand, website and know you how to create content but one question we haven't answered yet is.

How do all these things help me to get clients?

Make yourself comfy and grab a cup of tea as this is a big and complicated question. I will do my best to make this as easy as possible to understand. As you can imagine there's a lot to learn. I've studied this topic for more than 4 years and am continuously learning so condensing this and teaching you everything I know would take years. I don't believe in blueprints or formulas that guarantee you success. In my experience every business is as unique as the person behind it. What I can teach you is concepts and things that have worked for me and other practitioners. You can then pick and choose things that you want to do and that feel right for you and your business.

Most of us go into this line of work to help people and not to sell. Unfortunately, though in order to make a living you will have to sell your services. When I think of selling my first thoughts go to sleazy car sales men, telemarketers or people going from door-to-door trying to sell you something you really don't need. That just doesn't feel right and isn't aligned with living holistically and in harmony with the world around you and working towards the greater good.

Instead, think about selling your services and marketing as solving problems of people who desperately need exactly what you have to offer. If you genuinely come from a place of serving people and having their best interest at heart then the money will follow and your business will grow.

It takes time to build a sustainable business with a solid foundation. It's not enough to focus on marketing your business a couple of month of the year and once you see some results sit back and expect things to grow miraculously. It requires consistency. That doesn't mean you have to spend all day every day and thousands of Euro on it. Will it get you there faster if you did that? Maybe, but small consistent actions will get you there too. In fact, I believe that to grow a sustainable business it does take time and has certain stages of growth you have to go through that you can't rush. So many people spend time and money on things that just isn't right for their business at this moment and wonder why it doesn't work. Be consistent and show up and I promise you'll create momentum and clients will come.

A key ingredient to success is having a clear strategy and goals.

Setting realistic and measurable goals is a key element in making you successful. Don't expect that you'll make €1 million in the first year, grow your email list from 0 - 100,000 in 3 months. Instead, look at your current situation, how much time and effort you can put in and go from there. If you're starting from scratch maybe your goals will look like this:

•Grow your email list by 100 people in 3 months Grow your social media following by 250 people in 3 months

•Have x amount of appointments / people in a class Get 3 new clients per week

Once you have your goals you can create a plan of how to achieve them. You might have noticed that I like plans. Blame the German genes in me, but I like to be structured and have something to keep me on track.

It reminds me that I'm running a business and not following a hobby. A simple one page plan is enough, don't make it complicated. Like vision boards I like to create a yearly plan and then break it down into quarterly ones so it doesn't feel daunting to achieve them.

The main elements you want to cover in this plan are:

- Who are your clients? What do they need most? What services do you offer?
- What are your goals & timeframe to achieve them?
- What marketing channels do you use to get there?

So far we've covered everything but the last question. Marketing and the various channels have changed a lot over the years. When I was in college Social Media didn't exist. Can you imagine a world without Facebook or Instagram? A good place for advertising used to be the yellow pages. Now most households don't even have yellow pages anymore. My point is things change rapidly and platforms come and go. What is available now, might no longer be relevant in 5 years. For that reason, I won't be discussing each social media platform and how to use it, but teach you concepts that can be transferred to all different platforms including traditional marketing methods. A well-balanced mix of online and offline works best. Don't ignore them just because they feel old school. For holistic business in particular they seem to still work very well but together with the newer online channels.

A lot of people attempt doing it, but make one big mistake. They don't follow through and give potential clients exactly what they need. Let me explain in with the help of an example.

Say you are running a yoga workshop focusing on back bending. You have all the flyers done, social media posts and using all different channels to get people to book in. But when they click on the link you provide they're brought to the homepage, where there's no mention of the workshop and they have to go looking for the information. By that stage you've lost them. Only chance of converting them to customers is that they already know you and really really want to come to that workshop. Biggest mistake EVER.

If, however, you bring them in our workshop example to an event page that includes all the details they need including workshop dates, times and venue, how they'll benefit from attending this workshop as well as a link to book in and pay right there. Chances of them converting to customers and signing up to the workshop are significantly higher, because you're not leaving anything to chance. You're giving them exactly the information you promised and make it easy to sign up. They don't have to go looking for it, they don't have to email you to ask how to book in. Nothing. It's all already taken care of.

What your exact strategy looks like will depend on your clients, your business model but also on your own personal preference. Public speaking might be a great way for some but not for others. There's no point in forcing yourself to do something you're not comfortable with. Do you need to stretch your boundaries and start expanding them? Absolutely, but I believe that it's a slow process rather than jumping in the deep end. Don't stay in your comfort zone at all times. Test them, stretch and bend them and you'll be surprised what you're capable of. What I'm trying to say is that all of the things that I'm showing you the menu and it's up to you to pick the dish you like best. Don't feel like you have to do ALL of the things.

14

OFFLINE MARKETING

WE ARE SO CAUGHT up in the online world these days that we forget about all the traditional marketing tools. The internet has opened up the whole world and suddenly you can run a global business, while you're sitting at your kitchen table. BUT exactly that's the reason why offline methods will make a huge impression on your clients.

It can be slightly more expensive and depends a little bit on the type of business that you are running, but if you're for example in the holistic business and are seeing clients 1-to-1 or hold group classes it will work quite well.

Imagine finding a little inspirational note (with your details on the back) on a table of your favourite coffee shop? I promise you, people WILL look at it and if it interests them take it.

You can be as creative as you want with this. Start thinking outside of the box!

Marketing is all about connecting with your clients, serving them and making them feel valued. Let's dive in to the different forms of offline marketing.

Word of mouth marketing

Word of mouth marketing is still the easiest and most effective marketing tool for holistic businesses. People trust recommendations from people who have experienced a service more than any advertising out there. It's as easy as that. You are better of having a 100 people on your mailing list who absolutely LOVE everything you do and genuinely use your services and constantly tell everyone how great you are than 1000 people who just signed up, because you ran a competition to grow your list.

If you give them an amazing experience they will tell everyone they talk to about how great you are. This part is down to you. How can you make their experience special? Give them exactly what they need. It might be by providing them with outstanding customer service, little added bonuses they don't expect (think a tea & fruit while they're waiting for their treatment etc.) or even just being damn good at what you do and fixing whatever problem they come to you with. Give them the gift of you. Engage with them. Listen to what they are telling you.

You don't have to leave it up to chance for them to engage in conversations. Especially when you're starting out, tell them you'd love for them to tell their friends and family about your services if they've enjoyed it at the end of the session. You can even create a referral program to give them an incentive to come back as well as help you spread the word.

Things like:

- Share with your friends and get €10 off your next class/treatment

- Refer 5 people and get a free treatment/class
- Bring a friend to class and get your class free

You get the idea. Be creative. You can even advertise your referral program by adding it to your email signature. More to using all that in the online section of this chapter.

It means that sometimes you get requests from people who are not your ideal clients but over time you'll learn to recognise the signs and will be able to point them into directions of other practitioners who will be better suited for them. But even that will make an impression on them as it tells them you know who you are and what you're good. Rather than promising you can help them and not delivering as it's not exactly your area of expertise. They will appreciate your honesty on this.

Networking

Networking doesn't have to mean awkwardly standing in a room full of people trying to do small talk. Can you tell I'm an introvert and the thought of these networking events give me nightmares?

Networking happens every day all day. Every encounter with new people is a potential networking experience. They might not even be your target audience but know someone who is. Again, you don't have to come from the sales angle but from a genuine point of you. I regularly end up having conversations in coffee shops I work in with people. I don't have these conversations with the intention of selling them my service, but they just happen and usually the topic of what do you do turns up. I'm very passionate about everything I do and that comes across. When they're interested I either offer them my business card to leave the ball in their court or ask them if they want to give me their email address and I'll let them know about upcoming offers. It's that simple. Even as an introvert this is manageable.

Give yourself the challenge of telling someone about what you do every day. If you're feeling really brave set out to either ask 3 people a day for their email address or hand out business cards to them. It takes practice, but it helps in building your network and business profile.

Should you be someone who doesn't mind traditional networking events and coffee mornings, great! Go to them, but make sure that you the ones you go to have your ideal clients present. These meetings can be a great way to meet other entrepreneurs. 'Cause that's what you are. Like it or not. So even if your potential clients are not there they can be useful, as everyone has a network of their own. So whereas they might not use your services, they might know someone who will.

Flyers / Posters

You may not believe it, but flyers / posters are still a thing and still valuable. They might not work for other small businesses, but for holistic therapies they do. Especially when you combine them with the right timing. Just after Christmas is a great day to hand out flyers for fitness, pilates and yoga classes. Everyone is looking to better themselves come January 1st. Whether or not they'll stick with it is another question. The time leading up to Valentine's day is perfect for massage therapists. Every guy is looking for something to give their loved ones. Be smart about it. Other great places for posters are local health food stores, health conscious restaurants, coffee shops even hair dressers.

A little note on designing flyers. I would highly recommend outsourcing it to someone. For the simple reason that it will look more professional and will stand out from other posters/flyers around. Fiverr.com is always a good resource for it. Make sure to have all the information on it that people need. If your flyer is generic enough and doesn't have dates on them you can use them all year round or even for next year. Here are the basics:

1. What are you offering?
2. How to get in touch
3. Costs
4. Your website link
5. Logo
6. Short blurb about you including image
7. Call to action: Book now / Call now etc.

For printing check your local printers, but also online services like vistaprint.com. Compare prices. Proofread your flyer and make sure everything is correct. There's nothing worse than ordering a few hundred flyers only to realise you have a spelling error or even worse the wrong phone number on it. Get a second pair of eyes on it too if you can.

Talks / Information Events

Holding talks and information events to educate people about what you do is a great way of raising your profile. Some holistic therapies are new to people. They are unsure of what they are about, what they are for and whether or not they are for them. So not only are you educating people about what you do and get potential clients into a room, you also establish yourself as an expert. Sometimes Holistic Centres run open days you can be part of, reach out to health food stores, etc. If you are specialised on one area such as for example fertility, you can connect with GPs or fertility clinics. On that note, Building relationships with other people working in your speciality or potentially even partnering up with them is really beneficial. Referral programs work well here too.

Public Relations

While we're on the topic of raising your profile. Who says only big brands can get features and mentions in magazines, newspapers and radio? It is easier than you think. Most people just don't try. Running an event? Send a press release to your local news outlets. They are always looking to add events in. Getting a feature written about you and your work can be a little bit trickier and needs some more work. Journalists look for something unique and special. As soon as you have a unique spin to what you do, you have the best chances for it. Don't give up on this one. It might take a few attempts, but I know your story is worth sharing! While we're talking about print media I want to mention advertisements. Print advertising is extremely expensive and seeing the return on investment from them is nearly impossible. Some publications will create a so-called Advertorial which is a combination of an advertisement and an editorial or journalistic piece. They do work better, as people can get a feel for you and your services rather than just seeing an advertising among many others.

15

ONLINE MARKETING

TRADITIONAL OFFLINE MARKETING tools are often one way rather than 2-way communications. You talk to them but very rarely can they engage in conversations with you. In terms of marketing social media has been a game-changer. For the first-time people can interact and connect with businesses in real time. We sometimes forget the main elements of Social Media Networks. That is, they are designed to create a community (network) of like-minded people to be social and share common interests. For me there was a time that it has literally been a life saver while I was living abroad and working from home. I was able to connect with people all around the world on a daily basis. Unfortunately, nowadays we see the opposite happen. People getting more isolated, don't get out anymore and spend all their time on them without doing anything productively. That's a whole different conversation for another day though. From a business point of view a lot of people treat social media not for what they are but like any other traditional tool. Talking to people rather than communicating with them.

Social media works best as a marketing tool if you use it to build a community. Share useful information, tips, resources, links as well as answering questions and listen to what people want. Interact with your audience. Get them involved in your business. After all it's about THEM not you! Social media is not a quick fix that can catapult you to success. Not anymore. It takes time, effort and consistency to build a community. But slowly, over time, by sharing valuable information your audience, who by now you know really well, you build your profile and reputation as an expert in your field.

Emphasis on valuable information. Don't just sell to them. People get bored quickly with it and unfollow you. I use a simple 3-to-1 rule to make sure not to sell too much. For every promotional post you share you need to share 3 non-promotional pieces of information. That doesn't mean YOU have to create it all. You can if you want, but you can curate information too. I like a ratio of 70/30. 70% your own content 30% curated. Remember, the goal is to bring them back to your website for people to get to know YOU and your business not someone else's. But there is so much valuable content out there already that you'd be a fool not to use it. Specially if it comes from highly reputable sources such as medical journals, etc. You don't have to spend hours searching for it though. There are tools that do the job for you like:

http://trap.it/

https://feedly.com

https://contentgems.com/

While we're on tools, you already know I'm a fan of batching things like content creation, same is true for social media content. Spend an hour on a Monday morning or whenever suits you on creating and compiling the content for your social media and schedule it. Things like Hootsuite.com, buffer.com or postplanner.com are great tools for that. It saves you from stressing on a daily basis to create post social media content.

I want to make one thing clear though. You do NOT need to be on all social media platforms that exist. Think back to who your ideal clients are. Where do they hang out? Are they visual or text oriented? All these things factor in to what platforms you should use. Visual people probably won't be using Twitter and in reverse text-oriented people won't be interested in Instagram. Common sense, right?

Yet most people think they have to be on all or at least multiple platforms straight away. You'll be chasing your tail the whole time, trying to keep up with posting on many different platforms that you'll end up overwhelmed and ready to through all of it into the bin. You're better off being on one social media platform and mastering it and most of all using it to its full potential.

Use social media to share your story so that your clients can connect with it. Be your authentic, true self. That includes wins and successes but also a peak behind the curtain. What are you working on yourself? What are you struggling with? If you can get your clients to share their experience. Testimonials are the online version of word of mouth marketing.

Enough of talking theory though, let's take a look at an example of I would work a piece of content that I or a client of mine creates.

Again, you can do the pick and choose method, but in an ideal world I would personally do all of those things. Not that I do it currently 'cause you know nobody is perfect, but we can always aim towards it!

Of course, you can simply share the link with your audience. But there's so much more you can do with it.

Let's take a video as an example.

Re-purposing preparation

- Step 1.: You've either recorded a video or did a Facebook live.
- Step 2: Download the video and upload it to YouTube.
- Step 3: Send it to rev.com or fiverr.com to get transcribed. You can also use YouTube's inbuilt Subtitles/CC functionality. Only downside of this is that you have to edit out the timestamps which can be tedious.
- Step 4: Add Subtitles to your Video / Facebook live. In YouTube you just have to activate the feature. From there you can download the file and edit the Facebook Live video.
- Step 5: Extract audio from video.

You now have 3 different formats you can re-use and re-purpose from one single piece of content that probably didn't take you longer than 5-10 minutes to record. Crazy, right?

Create your blog post and add the video, audio as well as text in it as well as a call to action. (more to that as part of the Email section)

Re-purposing of the content

Text:

- Find short quotable sentences in your text and add a Click to Tweet feature into your blog (if you use Twitter that is...)
- Create beautiful branded graphics in Canva.com with the quote on it as well as the link to the blog and share on social media. If you mention any key influencers in the

video/post make sure to tag them as it will increase your reach.

- Create Pinterest suitable graphics from the quotes and title, add them to your Pinterest board.
- Re-write your post slightly in order to submit it to a relevant publication MindBodyGreen, Tinybuddha, Medium.com come to mind.
- Create an Infographic and share it on your social media.

Audio:

- Create a podcast from it that you submit to iTunes, Stitcher, Google Play Music.
- Create a SlideShare with the main points you've talked about and overlay it with your audio.
- Send it to your email list.

Video format:

If it makes sense from the content split it up into smaller videos and use it on other platforms such as Instagram.

You can see how one small video can create a ton of content that you can re-use. All those things link back to your original content on your website. What you're essentially doing is driving traffic to your website.

Now we need to convert them to either customers or future customers. Sometimes people are interested in your things, but aren't ready to join you for classes or book treatments. You wouldn't believe the amount of people who think about these things for months before finally taking the next step. What you do want to do is be on their radar and in the forefront of their minds when they are to take the next step. That's where your email marketing comes in and why it's so important to grow your list.

16

EMAIL MARKETING

THE FIRST HURDLE is getting them subscribed to your email list. The second to keep them engaged.

There was a time when it was enough to add a form on your website that said, 'Subscribe to our Newsletter'. Long gone are those times. People are less likely to just hand over their email address. They want to get to know you and your work before they pay for your services...Nowadays you have to bribe people. Although I don't like to use the word bribe. I rather see it as an exchange of energies and you giving them a sneak peak of how amazing you and your services are.

In the marketing lingo we call it a Freebie or Opt-in that you give people in exchange for their email address.

So, let's look at how we can create something of value to them that they actually need. A good freebie has the following 2 qualities:

It Must Provide a Solution to ONE Problem!

To be effective, your Freebie must solve that one incredibly annoying problem your ideal clients have... You're a pro at this by now and know this. It shouldn't be too hard to come up with something. But for good measure here are some examples:

Massage Therapists

- Problem: Neck and Shoulder Aches.
- Solution/Freebie: 5 Easy ways to get rid of Neck and Shoulder Ache in less than 10 minutes a day.

Yoga Teachers:

- Problem: Stress and the wish to calm down.
- Solution / Freebie: The Epic 5 Minute Calming Yoga Sequence you can do anywhere.

Quick & Easy to Implement

It's easy to think it needs to be something super elaborate and complicated...But honestly bigger is not always better...People don't have a lot of time to invest and want to see results fast. A one-page cheat sheet, a ten-minute audio file or a five minute video is enough. You're aiming for something that your they can instantly apply. Also choose the format that you and your clients are most comfortable with.

Here are some ideas:

- Free Challenge (like this one: christinejudd.com/challenge)
- Email/Video Series
- Access to a Group

- Audio Recording
- Printable/Checklist
- Mini Course
- eBook
- Sample of a bigger offer like a course
- Webinar

I recommend the 80/20 rule when it comes to your opt-in offer: spend 20% of your time creating your new offer, and 80% of it promoting it.

Don't over complicate things. You don't need a professional video set up to create videos, a smartphone and a tripod or selfie stick will do, or the voice recorder in your smartphone. To create cheatsheets you can either use Canva or get someone on Fiverr.com to design it for you which usually doesn't cost more than $5.

Do you see where I'm going with this? You want to create something that's easy for them to implement so they see quick results but good enough that they say. WOW! If that's her free stuff I wonder what her paid stuff is all about.

You've got the freebie, now what? You need to set it all up and connect your systems. Scary, I know but you can do it! You don't have to spend a fortune and it doesn't have to be hard to set up.

You'll need 3 things:

Email Marketing System

The easiest and most cost-effective system out there (in my opinion) is ActiveCampaign and they have great tutorial videos to set this up. It gives you the most user-friendly system and best follow up sequence options. If you're looking for a free tool you can check out Mailchimp.

Opt-in Form / Landing Page / Thank you page

People need to be able to sign up for your freebie. Thankfully technology makes this part so easy as most systems integrate with each other. There are two ways people can sign up for your freebie. From a form embedded in your blog post/your website and a Landing Page you direct people to. A landing page is a page that solely exists to capture your future client's information via a form. Only the information they are looking for is provided. No distractions, not even a navigation menu. The email address and other information you collect go straight into your email marketing system. No manual admin work required.

If you're using WordPress you can use a Plugin called Thrive Themes Architect. It's the easiest tool I have ever used for creating Landing Pages. You can even use it to create regular pages for your website. It's a simple drag and drop tool. It even lets you add an opt-in form to your blog posts. There are other tools out there such as Instapage.com and Leadpages that are free standing tools and don't require you to have a website.

Every landing page needs a thank you page. You don't want to let them hang dry, trying to figure out what to do next. Guide them through the process. Tell them what they should do now. You can either add the freebie download or video already on to the Thank You page. In which case that's all you have to do as they already get what they signed up for. Some countries require a double opt-in meaning after they've just signed up they need to re-confirm they really want your freebie. Annoying I know but it's the law. In this instance you'll need to tell them to 1) Check their email 2) Click the link to confirm their subscription 3) Access the freebie that we'll send you straight after that. Sound complicated I know and there are a lot of steps in this, but the systems make it really easy for you to do this. They have templates set up already where you just have to change the text. I like to send it to them via email as it gives you the first opportunity to establish a connection with them and educate them that you'll be coming in to their inbox from now on.

Nurture sequence.

You've got their email address and managed to deliver their promised freebie. Most people stop here and are losing out on a massive opportunity to build a relationship with that person and ultimately sell them something. You don't want to lead with that though. You wouldn't ask a stranger to go home with you after you just barely said hello. Let them get to know you. Tell them about who you are, what makes you tick, send them some even more valuable information (ideally relating to what they just got), what your clients say about you. Wow them by being your authentic, charming self.

What's next? Promoting, promoting, promoting. Here are a few ways of doing this

1. Share the link

Kind of a no-brainer, right? Simply share your Landing Page link with your friends, on your social media networks etc.

2. Add it to your email signature

Think about how many times you send emails to people? Every email is a prime opportunity to share your Freebie. If you use Gmail there's a neat little add on called Wisestamp. A free tool to create beautiful email signatures allowing you to add graphics that you can create for free in Canva.com

3. Add a pop up to your website

Reach more people by adding a pop up to your website. Again, there are some nice free tools you can use like Hellobar or Sumome. They are super easy to setup and give you tons of options.

4. Add the link to your Social Media Bios

The easiest way to share your Freebie is adding the link to your social media bios. Often the first place people look when they check you out.

5. Use your Cover Picture & 'Sign Up' Button on your Social Media Platforms

Your Facebook Cover picture is another prime location to make people aware of your free resource. You can link the 'Sign Up' button just below the cover image to your landing page.

6. Add the Freebie to your blog posts & sidebar

If you already have a blog on your website (if not get on it you should start one), make sure to add the nice graphic you made already to the sidebar linking to the landing page. In addition to this, you can add the same graphic to the end of your blog posts itself or link to a form directly.

You now have a process you can rinse and repeat any time you need. Some even say that you should create a different freebie for every blog post. Start with one though. Rome wasn't built in a day either. If all of this feels a bit too much for you right now and you don't know where to start with setting this all up, don't worry. I've got you covered with my own Freebie which has video tutorials included on how to manage the technical side of things. You can sign up to it at christinejudd.com/challenge. See what I'm doing here? Yup I'm giving you even more value and in return get your email address so I can stay in touch.

Keep the relationship you've built up with them by keeping in touch with them. Let them know what is going on with you and your business. Share your content with them, any special offers you have and be subtly in their mind for when they're ready to commit.

How often should you email them? Experts opinions vary on this one. I always say use common sense. How many times are you happy to receive an email from someone. How much is too much for you? You manage their expectations too. Send out an email every week or month on the same day. Your content should be so good they can't wait to open them!

17

GUEST POSTING

GUEST POSTING IS the public relations of the online world. We all need to create content, right? So do publications like Yoga Journal, MindBodyGreen, TinyBuddha, Huffington Post and all the others. That's where your expertise comes in. You have something unique to share. Prepare a well thought out written piece that gives their readers an insight into your world. The best pieces are always either giving them 'How to's they can easily implement or telling your story how you overcame an obstacle.

For example:

- *How to Make Progress On the Goals You're Tempted to Give Up On*
- *Attached to Your Smartphone? How I Overcame My Addiction*
- *4 Asana Sequencing Faux Pas That Leave You Feeling Blah*
- *15 Anti-Aging Health Benefits of Yoga That Will Make You Want to Start Practicing Now*

Some sites allow you to publish content that is already published somewhere else. Others want exclusive content. Be careful with choosing the publication as their readership needs to match your own audience. No point in putting in all the effort only to realise later that the people reading the site don't match your ideal client profile. Read their submission guidelines. Each site is different, but they will tell you exactly what they're looking for.

You already have a lot of ideas from creating your own content calendar. Go back and revisit it to see if something stands out to get published.

Why should you do this if you're running local classes and practices? To give you credibility, showcase your expertise and reach a wider audience. Once you're published you can add a 'As seen in' section with the publication logos on it. It does impress people and give them confidence seeing you're an expert and have contributed to big publications.

Using guest posting becomes even more useful when you start to offer information products like courses, books, etc. It's a way to reach a bigger audience with the least effort. Again like in your own blog you can incorporate a link to your own Freebie you created to bring them into your network to start giving them more value and sell them your virtual products.

All this is easier than you think and even if the first try doesn't get you published. Don't give up and get over the fear of rejection or even success. When I submitted my first article to the Huffington Post I was afraid, shaking even. Afraid of rejection, not being good enough. I did get accepted on the first try and the exhilaration I felt is indescribable. It becomes easier with time and the more you do it, the less of a big deal it is.

I know this chapter has a lot of information and can be overwhelming. What I want you to take away from it though is that consistently showing up with your marketing is the key. It doesn't matter how little or much you do as long as you're consistent. Consistency in my experience happens more often if you batch things and don't put yourself under pressure of creating something every day. Life gets busy and managing your social media and blog can get pushed down to the bottom of the to do list very quickly. Growing your business takes time and especially in the ever-changing social media world it takes time to build your following and reputation.

The second concept I want you to take away is that you don't have to do everything at once nor do you have to be everything for everyone. If you're starting out on social media and are nervous about technology, master one platform first and then move on to the next. You will grow more confident very quickly.

18

ALTERNATIVE INCOME STREAMS

RUNNING a holistic business brings its challenges. Unless you're running a yoga studio or holistic centre where you employ people you only have a certain capacity to take clients on. Meaning your income will be capped at some stage unless you either scale your business or take on additional avenues of income.

There are a lot of ways to make additional income. The easiest for holistic therapists to go with is selling products that complement their treatments such as creams, oils, etc. For yoga teachers you could sell mats, towels, blocks, essential oils etc. It does require you to manage stock, but if you're using the products already with your clients it can be a great way to add income.

Where my expertise comes in, however, is generating additional revenue through passive income. Imagine money coming in while you're sleeping? Passive income is the dream of (nearly) every entrepreneur.

Passive income can be as simple as selling printable & digital downloads such as eBooks for less than €10 or as elaborate as a video series & online courses for €500+.

The principle behind all of them is utilising and selling your knowledge to the world. You're not restricted to working with people in your area, but people from all over the world. You can reach and empower far more people with this than you can with giving treatments or teaching yoga classes locally. They can learn from the comfort of their home while you're making additional money.

How do you get people to buy your product? Having a great Marketing Funnel will ensure repeat clients and other income streams.

Basically, it means guiding your potential clients through the process of being becoming aware of you to becoming paying customers.

Here's what the typical marketing funnel looks like for the average holistic business owner:

- Step 1: Referral/marketing/advertising
- Step 2: Initial contact and call for services
- Step 3: Fee for Services (€50-200)

If you're lucky they continue to come to you.

This is a very limited approach to marketing as it's basically just trading money for time and doesn't include building long lasting relationships & trust with your clients. It also doesn't look at creating additional income streams for you establishing yourself as an expert.

In the ideal scenario you are guiding your ideal clients from free, to low cost followed by to higher valued services/products. Let them

get to know you and your value. Take a look at the more detailed
funnel below:

- Step 1: Referral/Marketing/Advertising Directed to your
  practice website
- Step 2: Opt in for free short report/e-book/video series
- Step 3: Consistent automated email follow up
- Step 4: Low-priced information products (e- books, cd's
  €10-15 range) info product leads to initial
  appointment/purchase (€75 -€200)
- Step 5: Educational email follow up sequence
- Step 6: Guide them to most deluxe package / repeat
  booking through follow up education (€2k and above)

Do you see how this will open you up to different income channels
and diversify your offerings? This works with both actual bookings
such as treatments as offers but even better with more information
products or online group programs.

It also helps to educate both current and prospective clients in an
automated fashion and helps you go away from just trading time for
money which will open you up to higher income.

The above example is quite a complex version, but start thinking of
creating at least the first 4 steps. You've already know how to create
your free opt-in, now you just have to create a low-cost offer. Make
no mistake though, low cost doesn't mean low value. You do need to
put effort and thought into these low-cost offers. Ideally it should
be something you could be selling at a higher price. You want to
WOW them and make them think ' If that's her free and low-cost
stuff imagine how her actual programs are?'

Every marketing funnel is a highly personal and unique aspect of your
practice and there are endless possibilities of what you can create.

Don't overthink it but keep it simple and here are some ideas for the different stages of your sales funnel:

- Freebies & Low-cost offers: e.g. eBooks, free audio, free video, blogs, quizzes & assessments etc.
- Programs: workshops, retreats, talks.
- Packages: a spring package, a flu package, a lower back pain package, a series or 3, 6 or 12 sessions etc.
- Here are the steps you need to take to create your first steps in your short funnel:
- Create an Opt-in offer
- Set up your opt-in form with your email provider & implement in your website
- Upload Opt-in to your Website or Dropbox
- Adjust the 'Welcome email' to add in your download link to Opt-in
- Create a Follow-up Series of emails in your email provider
- Offer them a low-cost product
- Create a Follow-up Series of emails in your email provider to educate them and lead to next higher priced products
- Create consistent contact, follow up and education

A lot of entrepreneurs, especially female, come up against massive money blocks around passive income. We're conditioned to think making money should be hard and requires sweat and tears. The thought of creating something once and then earning money from it on an ongoing basis can be alien and feel icky. But it's not different to authors making royalties of their books or singer/songwriters of their songs. It's just not as common in the holistic world. That doesn't make it wrong though, but requires mindset work to get over the blocks. Repeat after me: It is easy to make money. I am allowed to make money through passive income. I am worth it and can do it!

Don't get me wrong full passive income rarely exists, you need to put in the work to initially create it and then work on marketing to bring people to the products. But ultimately you will go from trading time for money business model to a sell-to-many concept. Reaching far more people, but taking up a lot less of your time.

19

TOOLS I CAN'T LIVE WITHOUT

AS AN ENTREPRENEUR you have to wear so many hats, that it can be difficult to manage all the information and content you require on a daily basis. Let's face it. Admin is the biggest pain of running your business. I have met very few people actually enjoy doing their admin work. Thankfully there are some smart tools out there that will make your life a lot easier and reduce the time you spend on administrative work.

We've already mentioned some of them but I wanted to go through my favourite ones and show you how I use them.

Accounting:

Waveapps.com

I can't recommend this tool enough. If you're still managing your invoicing with Word or Excel. Go get this tool now! It's free to use!

I know invoicing and bookkeeping can be a really difficult and annoying part of my business. With tools like this it will get slightly easier. You can store client information in it, different services and their pricing and can whip out an invoice in less than a minute.

It gets even better. You can upload your receipts straight from a phone app and have it all together to hand over to your accountant.

How amazing is that? I'm by no means paid by them to say this, but I simply find this tool so valuable that I always recommend it. There are other tools out there including FreshBooks, QuickBooks, Xero and many more.

Payment

Making it easy to get paid is so important and will help you get more clients. Easiest and most common tool for this is PayPal. Secure and easy to use. You can integrate it into your website and even get a link you can send people to.

Another option I like is Stripe. It integrates with a lot of other tools, but some not as easy as PayPal.

20

BOUNDARIES

I WANT to talk a little bit about boundaries. They're so important, yet so hard to establish.

Starting to see your business grow is amazing.

You FINALLY begin to see all the hard work pay off. People are contacting you for business and existing clients want more work done.

When first establishing your business, you're likely to move heaven and earth to fulfill your clients' requests. You'll be working and answering phones and messages evenings, nights and weekends out of fear of losing out on business; at least I did.

Once your business starts growing you will have to start to put boundaries in to place and manage expectations of your clients. What are your business hours? How should your clients get in touch with you? Are WhatsApp & messenger or texts really the best way to manage your communications with your clients? What's your response time?

Sound familiar? Believe me I know how you feel! Your partner won't be happy if you start working at 12am on a Saturday night. If you don't believe me ask mine. He'll be able to tell you a few stories.

I know it's easy to think that you have to be available 24/7 to clients and that you need to answer clients or prospects straight way or your business will fail! I PROMISE you that you don't!

Is your GP or any other established company available 24/7? No, unless they have a dedicated support team available, they don't.

Does it mean that people won't do business with them? No, because they've managed expectations and you know when you'll approximately receive a reply.

Here are a few simple things you can do to set boundaries in your business and set yourself up for success.

SET UP TERMS & CONDITIONS - PUBLISH THEM ON YOUR WEBSITE AND NOTIFY YOUR CLIENTS

This is so important and yet most people don't have them in place! I'm guilty of not having them in place up until now as well! Mea culpa! How are your clients supposed to know where your boundaries are? What's acceptable and what's not? We've already covered this earlier, but it's so important you do have them and communicate them.

Yes, it's difficult to communicate that to your existing clients, but keep it short and sweet. Just let them know you're updating your terms and conditions and wanted to communicate it to them. No need to elaborate and justify yourself.

GET A BUSINESS PHONE

Starting out in your business there's no need to get a special phone JUST for your business. I honestly recommend that you do! Keeping your personal and business communications separate will not only avoid late night phone calls from clients, it will also make it easier for your finances.

USE EMAIL AS PRIMARY COMMUNICATION METHOD

In the world of Facebook messenger and other messenger apps, it's such an easy thing to NOT do. Chatting to people is fast and easy, but you'll see that not only will it suck up a lot of your time, but if you have apps on your phone you'll catch yourself answering messages at all hours of the day.

SET UP AN AUTORESPONDER

A great way to manage expectations with future and current clients is to set up an autoresponder from your email. Tell them that their email has landed safely in our inbox and let them know when they can expect a response. Do you get the same questions asked all the time? Answer them in your autoresponder too or redirect them to a page on your FAQ page on your website.

Keeping private and business life separate is difficult specially as a solopreneur. Your work is your life. But if you're in it for the long haul, you need to set clear boundaries for your own sanity.

Setting up boundaries for me has been the most challenging part of running a business. Getting clients? Easy. Creating a website? Easy peasy compared to setting boundaries. I'm a people pleaser and a lot of holistic practitioners are too, but remember you can't give from an empty cup. Self-face is so important for an Entrepreneur.

If you're constantly exhausted and starting to feel resentful of clients who overstep your boundaries you need to rethink your approach. Have you communicated your boundaries clearly? If no, then it's time to do so. If they're still overstepping your boundaries it might be time to part with those clients.

21

DEALING WITH OVERWHELM

ONCE BUSINESS IS BOOMING and you're getting busy it's easy to feel overwhelmed. I want to share with you some strategies that have helped me to manage the overwhelm and ultimately reduce it. Overwhelm usually comes from not managing your time and resources most effectively. You're stretching yourself too thin and are trying to do too much.

BATCH CLIENT APPOINTMENTS/CLASSES

This is a really good one, but also difficult one. I've learnt the lesson the hard way. It's not even funny how much time and energy I have wasted running around during the week running all over the city to teach different classes, attend meetings as well serve my massage clients. It also drains your energy and adds to the overwhelm.

I see this most often with yoga teachers. Most have to teach several classes in different locations, often in the same day. In the long run this is not sustainable. Trying to batch classes in the same area for the same day ultimately is the key to this. Granted, it's not a quick fix and will take some time to put in place. Take a look at your classes. Are there any that you're doing that are out of your way that aren't making you any profit? Might be time to let those go and look to establish other new classes around the ones that do work within the vicinity.

Same goes for any other business. Can you batch your appointment schedule so you don't have a client first thing in the morning and another late at night?

SCHEDULE IN DOWNTIME

We all know how important self-care is, yet it's the last thing we usually make time for. There's always something to do, a class to teach, a client to attend to, a blog post to write or doing admin stuff. But for any entrepreneur scheduling downtime should be a non-negotiable item on your to do list. If you have to block out time in your calendar that is reserved for self-care. Be strict about it. Don't give in and let a client book in an appointment during that time. You're simply not available. It can be an hour in your day, a few hours once a week or even a full day. In fact, I want you to go ahead right now and do it. Schedule time for a bath, a visit to your favourite coffee shop with a good book or just take a nap! Report back how it felt!

SAY NO TO CLIENTS

Yes, its counter-intuitive. You're running a business so why should you say no to clients? It's about only taking on as much work as you can handle. That's especially tricky when you're just starting out. I used to think that I need to take on every single project that presented itself. The end result? A bucket load of work and total overwhelm. So, check in with yourself before taking on more clients.

And just for full disclosure, all of these things are work in progress for me and need constant reinforcement. So don't beat yourself up if it takes a while to implement.

KEEP ON TOP OF YOUR EMAILS

Email has become such an important part of our life that we feel lost without it. The amount of emails some people receive are unimaginable. I know people in corporates who get hundreds, if not thousands of emails a day. Imagine that amount in actual letters!

I want you to stop letting emails rule your life and ruin your day. You might not even realise how much stress your inbox is causing you.

Guess what? You DON'T have to answer every email instantly!

I want to give you some practical tips on how to organise your emails so you have the bare minimum in your inbox, namely those that need attention that same day!

Here is what I want you to do!

Schedule an hour each day for the next week to start organising your inbox(depending on how many emails are in your inbox)

I know this sounds a lot but I PROMISE it's worth it. Here are the rules!

Keep in your inbox:

- Messages that you haven't read yet.
- A limited number of messages that need prompt attention.

File away:

- Anything that you've dealt with in the past 30 days, but may still be important or have information you want to remember/conversations you want to track.

Delete:

- Anything over 30 days that you haven't touched and doesn't contain any SUPER important info, any promotional emails you no longer need.

STEP 1:

Declutter your subscriptions

We have a tendency to subscribe to a lot of programs, newsletters. Time to declutter and organise. Be ruthless! Chuck anything out that you no longer need. You will feel liberated!

Thankfully you don't have to go in to each individual one and unsubscribe you can just use a tool to organise them for your and get a daily or weekly digest of them.

Unroll.me: This handy helper "rolls up" emails that you receive often into one digest that you can receive at specified time of day. It starts by identifying emails in your inbox that you get often, and allows you to unsubscribe right from the service, add to your roll up, or keep in your inbox. It's also a lifesaver for personal email.

STEP 2: CREATE YOUR EMAIL FILING SYSTEM

A filing system is helpful for organizing emails so that if you need to go back to something, you can quickly find it. It also helps to keep important emails that you're currently dealing with from being lost in the shuffle!

QUICKLY SCAN YOUR EMAILS AND CREATE A LIST OF

"BIG" CATEGORIES. FOR INSTANCE:

- Come back to
- Customers
- Suppliers
- Marketing
- Admin
- Programs
- Come back to

Create folders for each of the categories and any subcategories if you need them. It's time to start filing your emails!

STEP 3: CREATE RULES

Creating Rules for emails that you want to keep but that you don't need to action should bypass your inbox. Think of newsletters, Facebook notifications, PayPal notification and LinkedIn group updates etc.

Create rules to get them filed, and they'll skip your inbox all together!

Rules allow you to identify emails by sender, subject line, or recipient, and then have a specific action performed. For example, you can create a rule that any bills you have set up for auto-pay get sent directly to your Accounts Payable folder, so you can review them when you have a minute – and they're not in your face.

Another way to use rules is to send emails from your customers straight in to their respective folder so you can action them when you are working on their project - I tend not to have more than 20 actionable emails in my inbox!

It feels like a daunting task, I know! But the relief you will experience once you're done is exhilarating!

22

THE IMPORTANCE OF INVESTING IN YOUR BUSINESS

WHEN STARTING we like to pretend we're superheroes! Juggling a million things at once, thinking we have to do them all ourselves. Sometimes we have to admit that we are not superheroes and that we need help. There's no shame in it and investing in yourself and your business will pay off EVERY SINGLE TIME.

After all, you went down this path to have more freedom in your life and doing the things you love. Sometimes that means getting help with the things you're not good at. Your business can't grow without help & investment. That's a fact. Be it in form of tools to make your life easier, help with things like accounting or social media management or even a coach. If you want to grow your business and create financial freedom you need to spend more time doing what you're good at and letting go of the things you're not. Letting go of control is difficult. It's easy to think that no one can run your business better than yourself. It's your baby that you have built up from the ground and you know it inside and out. But think about it for a minute. There is a reason companies employ people for different things. They're specialised in it. Just like you're a specialist in your own holistic therapy or yoga, there are people out there specialising in things you need to run a business effectively. You can and should take up those resources. That doesn't mean you have to employ a full-time person. Outsourcing things can be as simple as hiring a bookkeeper a couple of hours a month to manage your accounts, an accountant once a year to submit your tax return, a virtual assistant a few hours a week helping you with either admin or social media, a cleaner or anything else that sucks up your precious time. Those freed up hours are hours you can spend doing things that earn you money.

One of the reasons not to invest, whatever form that may take, is money. Spare cash is rare in the beginning of a business and often we don't make investments, because we think we don't have the money. I get it. I've been there and have used the same excuse. 'Cause that's what it is in my experience. The Universe always provides and the money appears once you make the decision to take that step.

Think about it. How many hours do you spend on the things you don't enjoy and are not good at? How much do you make per hour and how much will it cost you to outsource these things? If you're making more money than it costs you to hire someone, it's time to outsource.

23

THANK YOU!

I WANT to thank you once again for picking up this book and reading it till the end. There's a lot of information compressed in these pages. I hope you found it useful and were able to pick up things how you can run your business or maybe make it a little more effective. Please don't expect that you will have everything I talk about in this book figured out or implemented straight away. Some of the things take time and are a constant challenge for us all. So please don't beat yourself up over it and don't attempt to do it all at once. Maybe pick one thing at a time and work on it consistently rather than spreading yourself thin and trying to do it all. Start outsourcing things that are not in your zone of genius. It's OK to ask for help.

The last piece of wisdom I want to give to you before I send you off on your way to success is to find a network of like-minded people in the same situation. Partners, family and friends often don't understand what entrepreneurs go through or sometimes even what we do. The up and downs we have to endure, the stress and even sometimes the loneliness of running your own business. Having a circle around you who know what you're talking about and who understand you without having to say much is priceless.

BONUS TRAINING

This book will provide you will everything you need to know to set up and run your holistic business. I know that sometimes translating the theory into practice can be hard, especially when it comes to figuring out systems and technology such as email marketing systems.

I believe building your email list is one of THE most important things you can do, which is why I want to give all my readers a special bonus.

I've created an exclusive video course on email marketing just for you. The videos take you step-by-step through everything you need to know, starting with which system to use, how to come up with a freebie to give subscribers in exchange for their email addresses to actually creating that freebie and setting it up in your system. You can claim your bonus from the link below.

http://christinejudd.com/bonus

Make sure to send me links to all your freebies as I always love to see what you create! hello@christinejudd.com

ABOUT THE AUTHOR

Christine Judd is a holistic business mentor, author, yoga teacher and Lomi Lomi practitioner. She's passionate about helping holistic practitioners reach their potential by building sustainable businesses they love. By bringing marketing and technology together, Christine helps fledgling business owners get focused on what they want to do, while putting systems in place that make running their business (and life) simpler.

Get your bonus material here:
christinejudd.com/bonus/
hello@christinejudd.com